D1760789

PENGUIN BOOKS
A PARENT'S GUIDE TO HELPING WITH MATHS

Diana Kimpton was born in London in 1949. She special-
ized in maths and science at school and went on to gain a
first-class honours degree in maths at Reading University.
After training as a teacher, she taught in Britain and in
Nigeria.

She gave up full-time teaching when her first son was
born but continued to teach children maths on a one-to-
one basis. While she was helping her daughter, some
parents asked how they could help their children too and
the idea for this book was born.

Diana Kimpton's first book, *A Special Child in the Family*,
was for parents of sick or disabled children. Her other
work includes *The Hospital Highway Code* which she wrote
for children in hospital and the picture book *The Bear
Father Christmas Forgot*.

She enjoys horse-riding and amateur dramatics.

A Parent's Guide to Helping with Maths

Diana Kimpton

PENGUIN BOOKS

PENGUIN BOOKS

Published by the Penguin Group
Penguin Books Ltd, 27 Wrights Lane, London W8 5TZ, England
Penguin Books USA Inc., 375 Hudson Street, New York, New York 10014, USA
Penguin Books Australia Ltd, Ringwood, Victoria, Australia
Penguin Books Canada Ltd, 10 Alcorn Avenue, Toronto, Ontario, Canada M4V 3B2
Penguin Books (NZ) Ltd, 182–190 Wairau Road, Auckland 10, New Zealand

Penguin Books Ltd, Registered Offices: Harmondsworth, Middlesex, England

First published 1995
10 9 8 7 6 5 4 3 2 1

Filmset by Datix International Limited, Bungay, Suffolk
Printed in England by Clays Ltd, St Ives plc
Set in Monophoto Bembo

For Melissa
who taught me so much while I was teaching her

Contents

Acknowledgements

My grateful thanks go

to *Andrew, Flick, Karen and Steve* for all their encouragement and for valiantly acting as guinea-pigs by reading the first draft;

to *Gwen Hart* for passing on the secret of the quick way to multiply by nine on your fingers;

and to *Paul, Matthew and Melissa* for putting up with their mum spending so much time in front of a word processor.

Introduction

Does your child find maths difficult? Do sums cause tears? Then this book is for you. With its guidance, you can give your child the one-to-one help he or she needs but which is so rarely available in school. I've developed this approach from my own experiences as a mathematician, as a teacher and, most importantly, as a parent. I am not claiming it's the only way to teach maths but it's a way that works and which can be used at home by anyone with patience and some time to spare.

Unfortunately the English language lacks one word to use instead of he and she, and the modern alternatives of s/he and he/she don't fit easily into my style of writing. This faced me with a dilemma. If I used he throughout, would I perpetuate the misconception that maths is only important for boys? If I plumped for she instead, would I be encouraging the equally mistaken belief that girls are no good at maths? Whichever I chose, would I be risking antagonizing half my potential readers and their children?

I finally settled on using he and she in alternate chapters. This is as near as I can get to trying to please everyone. I hope it works for you.

How to Use This Book

Section 1 explains how and why this system works. It's vital that you understand this, so please read the whole section *before* you start to help your child.

Section 2 contains all the basic number skills your child must have to succeed in maths. Work through the whole section from beginning to end, even if your child says she knows it all already. The extra practice will improve both her confidence and her competence and you'll be able to spot any gaps in her knowledge which you need to fill.

Section 3 contains a selection of other mathematical topics your child may meet. As the order in which these topics occur varies from school to school, this section is *not* designed to be worked through from beginning to end. Instead you can dip into it as and when you need to. There are clear guidelines to make sure you don't tackle a topic until your child has the right background knowledge.

1 / What's Wrong with Maths?

In most school subjects the order you learn topics isn't really important. In geography you can study Australia before or after you tackle France and, in history, it's perfectly possible to learn about the American War of Independence without having a clue what Columbus was up to in 1492.

But maths is different as each new topic builds on previous ones. If you haven't got all the necessary background knowledge, learning something new is as hard as trying to build a tower when some of the bottom bricks are missing.

There are many reasons why your child may not possess as much background knowledge as his maths teacher expects. Perhaps he was away when a particular topic was taught or his ability to learn was affected for a while by an emotional upset such as bullying or the death of the family cat. Perhaps he has been faced with worksheets he couldn't read easily or been given too little practice to enable him to master new skills. Whatever the reason, the problem is still the same: he has been taught maths faster than he has learnt it.

There is only one way to deal with this situation. You must fill in the missing gaps in his knowledge, starting with the ones which cause the most trouble: the gaps in his basic number skills. These skills are vital because they form the foundation for the rest of maths. Unless your child can add, subtract, multiply and divide, he can't solve equations, work out percentages or fully understand timetables and the twenty-four-hour clock. Although calculators have taken much of the drudgery out of long calculations, they haven't removed the need for your child to be able to understand and use numbers competently.

But my child isn't just bad at maths. He finds all his school work difficult.

It would be a good idea to find out if there is some underlying cause for his problems. Have his vision and hearing checked and ask the school to arrange for him to see an educational psychologist who can test for specific learning difficulties. The sooner such problems are spotted, the sooner he can start to receive the right help. Whatever the results of these investigations, you can still continue to help him with maths yourself.

2 / Can Parents Help?

Don't worry. You don't need to be a teacher or a mathematician before you can help your child with maths. You have other advantages to offer. You know your child far better than any teacher and you've already helped her learn many things. Remember, it was you, not the school, who taught her to speak and to feed herself.

But one of the biggest advantages you have is that you're not trying to help twenty or thirty other children at the same time. Close your eyes for a minute and imagine a maths lesson. The children are bent eagerly over their work while the teacher walks round giving a little extra explanation here, a slight encouragement there.

Come on! You can do better than that. Think back to your own school-days and add a little realism. Suddenly the noise level in the classroom rises. Two small boys at the back start to fight over a pencil. Several hands go up and their owners announce 'I've finished, I've finished.' The teacher rushes to give them extra work before their eager minds find more mischievous occupations. A book crashes to the floor as the pencil fight reaches a crescendo and a cry of 'I feel sick' comes from a pale girl in the front row.

Now in the midst of all this activity, put one quiet girl. She holds her pencil but she doesn't write. There are numbers on the page: sums. She doesn't know what they mean but she knows that if she tries to do them she'll get crosses. She hates crosses. She hates numbers. She's sure there's no point in asking for help because she knows she's stupid. Her mental shutters come down and she stares out of the window.

Bearing in mind everything else which is going on, it's hardly surprising that her teacher can't manage to spend more than a short time with her: time for a brief explanation or a few words of encouragement but not long enough to undo the damage caused by weeks or months of failure.

It's getting depressing, isn't it? Let's change the fantasy and imagine that same girl at home where she feels safe and secure. She's sitting at a table with her dad. Just as before, she has a pencil in her hand and a page of sums in front of her but this time the work is within her capabilities. Even so, she panics at the sight of it because she has failed so much in the past. But her dad knows her well enough to recognize her fear. He reassures her that she can manage, works with her until she gains confidence and gently ensures that she gets each sum right. A smile lights her face at the sight of her page of ticks and a gold star.

That may sound too good to be true but it isn't: I've seen it happen. But don't get the wrong idea. It's not easy to combine the role of parent and teacher. In my experience, it's not easy to combine the role of parent with anything – parenting is hard work. Helping your child with maths will take time and effort but it's something you *can* do.

But I'm hopeless at maths myself.

You don't need to be a mathematical genius to help your child, but it's certainly useful if you know more than she does. If you've little confidence in your own ability with numbers, work through Section 2 on your own or with the help of a friend. You don't have to finish the whole scheme before you begin to work with your child but try to keep a few sessions ahead.

If you practise like this beforehand, you don't need to keep it secret. Admitting that you find maths difficult too can make your child feel less embarrassed about her own problems. You can even turn tackling arithmetic into a team effort by letting her use a calculator to mark your work.

But maths has changed since I was at school.

Maths changes all the time. Fresh discoveries add new bricks to the top of the tower of knowledge. Pythagoras may have been good with right-angled triangles but he wouldn't have had a clue how to tackle integral calculus. Fashions in teaching alter the range of topics taught at school: out goes formal geometry, in come transformations and vectors.

But basic arithmetic (or number work) stays the same year after year. Two plus two is four whether you're counting dinosaurs or intergalactic space shuttles.

Your child is learning the same basic skills as you did but she may not be taught them in the same way. At relevant stages of the book, you'll find explanations and advice to help you avoid the cry 'My teacher doesn't do it like *that*!'

But won't I increase the pressures on her if I try to help her at home?

Your child's problems with maths come from trying to learn work which is too difficult. If you just give her more work which is too hard, you definitely will increase the pressure on her and confirm her feelings of failure.

But using this book to help your child will not have that effect. Instead of asking her to do the impossible, you're going back to the beginning of maths so she has another chance to learn those vital basic skills properly. As she succeeds, numbers will make more sense and the pressure will lessen.

But I get so cross with her when she doesn't understand.

Yelling at your child doesn't help her to learn. Neither does telling her to pull herself together or suggesting she stops being so stupid. In the same way, saying 'hurry up' or drumming your fingers impatiently on the table are more likely to make her panic than make her work faster.

Patience is the number one virtue for parents and teachers but we're all human beings, not angels. I know only too well how easy it is to lose your temper when you watch your child struggle with an apparently easy question, especially if you've also had a bad day at work and the plumbing's gone wrong. But for your child's sake, it's much better if you can take a deep breath and deliberately speak quietly as you encourage her through this tricky patch. In other words – when you can't *be* patient, you must try to *act* patient.

If you really have no patience at all and you're a bad actor, you may not be the best person to help your child with maths. Perhaps you could ask a friend or relative to use this book to help her instead.

The school say I should leave it to them to help her.

You obviously don't want to antagonize the school unnecessarily but you've been leaving it up to them so far and look where that has got her. If the school is only going to continue teaching her the same way as before, start to help her anyway. The methods I suggest fit in well with any teaching she may be having at school and the extra practice can't do any harm. Her teachers' objections are likely to lessen when they see her work improve.

Of course, it may be that she's just changed schools or has a new teacher. In that case, you may decide to give the professionals another chance but don't wait too long. If her maths hasn't improved in a few weeks, start to help her yourself anyway.

DON'T FORGET
- You *can* help your child
- You know your child better than the teachers do
- If you're not happy with maths yourself, work through the scheme first, staying a few steps ahead of your child

3 / How This System Works

This method of helping your child isn't just a matter of giving him a few extra sums to do while you tackle the ironing. Instead you're going to give him your total undivided attention throughout each session. That's what makes the system work.

This technique is quite different from the class teaching your child gets at school. It's also much more intensive and tiring for both of you: that's why the sessions are short.

Thinking about Maths

The first part of each session is for oral work or mental arithmetic. This will range from straightforward counting work to practising multiplication tables and working out small problems. These apparently simple exercises work in a similar way to the warm-up routines used by athletes. They develop mental agility and confidence, preparing your child's mind for the harder work which is to follow.

Writing Maths

Mental ability with numbers is important but it isn't enough. To succeed at school, your child also needs to be able to tackle written questions with confidence. That's why he will be doing some written work in the second part of each session. This emphasis on 'sums' may look old-fashioned but the regular practice will improve both his confidence and his ability.

Flexibility

The big advantage of this system is that it's totally flexible. Because you're going to create your own maths exercises designed especially for your child, the work you give him will always be exactly right for the learning stage he's reached. You can adjust the length of the exercises to suit the speed at which he works and make sure he has as much practice as he needs before he moves on to the next step.

Don't panic! Writing exercises is nowhere near as hard as it sounds. Each new topic is divided into a number of small steps and, for each step, you'll find a sample exercise plus detailed instructions on how to write extra ones if you need them.

Building Confidence

The trouble with maths is that you can get it totally and completely wrong and there are few things as discouraging as a page of crosses (except, of course, a whole exercise book of crosses). Fortunately the opposite is true too. It's possible to get maths completely right and a page of ticks is a tremendous confidence booster.

To make sure you fill all the gaps in your child's knowledge, you're going to go right back to the beginning of maths and work through each topic again. By returning to very easy work, you'll make sure your child succeeds in that first session you spend together. As you progress through the work in small steps at your child's pace, you'll be able to keep him succeeding even while he's learning new skills. This constant success will build your child's confidence with numbers at the same time as he learns the skills he needs.

But surely he'll make mistakes?

Of course he will but mistakes don't have to turn into failure.

Because you're with him all the time he's working, you can step in as soon as he goes wrong and suggest he tries again. Since you never mark the questions until he has got them right, he'll never get any crosses.

Won't he get bored if he's doing work he already knows?

No, because he won't be doing it for very long. If he already knows a topic well, he can move quickly on to the next one.

DON'T FORGET
This system is based on:
- **short sessions**
- **individually designed exercises**
- **success**

---

4 / Gaining Your Child's Cooperation

Do you remember when you were at school? There was a definite feeling of them and us. Whether you loved, hated or feared your teachers, they were on the other side of the divide: people who made you sit when you wanted to run, be quiet when you wanted to shout and work when you wanted to play.

Although teaching methods have changed since then, the them and us attitude hasn't. Your child will probably resist your efforts to help her if she thinks you're ganging up with the teachers. She's much more likely to cooperate if she feels you're on her side. And gaining her cooperation is vital. Without it, your sessions together will become a battleground instead of a pleasant learning experience.

Showing You Understand

Once you know or suspect that your child is finding maths difficult, find a suitable time to talk to her about it. This needs to be relaxed and unrushed so don't choose a moment just before you have to go out or when her favourite TV programme is about to start.

Bring up the subject of maths gently and be prepared for tears, anger or attempts to change the subject. If necessary, spread the introduction of the ideas in this chapter over several short chats instead of covering them all in one marathon discussion.

As soon as you start talking about maths, make it clear that you're not criticizing her efforts and you're not angry about her inability to cope with the work. Let her know that you understand how dispiriting it is to find something really hard. Tell her how fed up you felt when you were struggling to learn a subject you didn't understand. (I bet there was one: with me it was French.) Try using phrases like 'Isn't it horrible when teachers shout at you?' or 'I hated it when the whole class knew I got it all wrong'. Such comments put you firmly on your child's side.

Giving Hope

Reassure her that many people find maths hard and that failing to understand something straight away doesn't mean she is stupid, lazy or useless with numbers. Neither does it mean that all's lost and she'll never understand. I can still remember writing nine thousand, nine hundred and three as 90009003 and soaking my book with tears when I first tried algebra but I eventually understood it all well enough to obtain a first-class honours degree in maths.

Explaining What's Gone Wrong ·

Now explain to your child that she finds maths difficult because she's been taught it faster than she has learnt it. (Remember to say it this way round.) I find the easiest way to explain it is to compare maths to a tower of bricks. You can build a real tower to illustrate what you're saying if you like but it isn't essential.

Talk about the way one new topic in maths builds on another just like the bricks in a tower. If there's a brick missing, all the bricks above it have nothing to sit on so they fall down. In the same way, if she's got a gap in her maths knowledge, she can't learn the topics which build on it.

Even when all the bricks are there, the tower will wobble if the bricks aren't placed squarely on each other and trying to add one more brick can make the whole tower collapse. In the same way, even if she hasn't got any obvious gaps in her knowledge, your child will find it more and more difficult to learn new topics in maths if her knowledge of the earlier ones is shaky.

Offering to Help

Once she's sure you're on her side and understands why she's having problems, you can offer to help her put back the missing bricks or reposition the wobbly ones so she can do better at maths. Your suggestion may be greeted with relief and enthusiasm but don't be surprised if it's not. Here are some of the most likely doubts she may have and some hints on how to counteract them.

You don't know how to do it.

Yes, you do. You've got this book to help you. Let her look at it if she wants to. There's nothing to hide.

It won't work. I'm too bad at maths.

No one is too bad to help. You're not promising to turn her into a genius, but you can definitely help her improve.

If she's still unconvinced, try making a deal: you'll help for three months. Then, if she hasn't improved at all, you'll stop if she wants you to.

I don't want to do extra work at home. It takes too much time.

This type of help doesn't take hours and hours of work each week. None of the sessions needs to be longer than twenty minutes and you can make them shorter if you wish. Decide on mutually agreeable times which don't interfere too much with her social life, hobbies and TV programmes. Keep enough flexibility in the system to cope with occasional events like birthday parties.

I'll be teased at school if the other children know my mum's helping me.

No one else needs to know unless she wants them to. Talk together about whether your help should be a secret. Does she mind if you tell *your* friends what you're doing? Can you tell grandma or her teacher? Perhaps she'd like it to stay secret until everyone can see how much better she's doing.

Keeping Up Her Interest

Gaining your child's cooperation before you start to help her is only part of the battle. You've also got to encourage her the whole time you're working together or she may feel dispirited and give up. This is particularly important in the early stages when the work you're doing may not be directly relevant to her schoolwork.

Praise is one way to give her the encouragement she needs but beware of praising everything she does indiscriminately. If you do, she'll soon decide your praise is worthless and it'll cease to have any effect.

To avoid this trap, use different levels of praise ranging from nods and smiles, through 'that's right' and 'good' to 'that's terrific' and 'congratulations'. Save the greatest praise for her greatest efforts and achievements and make your praise specific. 'I'm really pleased at how much neater your work is today' can allow her to glow with satisfaction even on a day when she knows she's had to struggle to get the right answers.

The other extremely effective way to encourage your child is with a system of rewards. The power of the gold star is enormous. That's why generations of teachers have used it. A gold star is a concrete symbol of success. I've seen children's faces light up with joy at receiving one. I've seen fifteen-year-olds on probation work feverishly to get one. But don't feel you must use stars just because I do. If you know something else your child would prefer, then use it.

The only problem with giving rewards is that the absence of them reinforces failure. That shouldn't be a problem as this system of helping with maths makes sure your child always succeeds. Of course, the effect of the rewards drops gradually if she keeps getting them but changing the reward on offer can often restore its effectiveness. As the novelty of the gold stars wears off, try giving tokens which can be exchanged for extra pocket money, comics or similar treats.

Avoiding Discouragement

Try to avoid the temptation to introduce time pressures and competition into your sessions. Although it might sound fun to turn an exercise into a race, races have winners and losers and losing won't improve your child's confidence.

It's particularly important to avoid competition with any other children you know who are working through this same scheme. Please don't start thinking, let's try to finish chapter 12 before Jonathan. If you do, you risk rushing your child through the work too fast instead of letting her work at her own pace.

DON'T FORGET
- **Show you're on your child's side**
- **Explain why she's having problems**
- **Make sure sessions don't clash with other activities**
- **Don't mention your help without your child's permission**
- **Make your praise specific**
- **Give rewards**
- **Don't introduce competition**

---

5 / Before You Start

Mathematics is much easier to learn if you can relate it to the real world. For number work, that means having real objects to count. You could use small building bricks, matchsticks or buttons but they all have one major disadvantage: no one normally counts them. If your child considers such learning aids childish, asking him to use them will inflict yet more damage on his already battered self-confidence.

However you already have the perfect solution in your pocket: money. Coins are supposed to be counted so always have some available during your maths sessions. Your child sees adults count them in shops and banks so he knows it's a real task, not an artificial one for 'babies'.

Money has another big advantage over buttons or bricks. It's a very effective way of illustrating place value (hundreds, tens and units) without investing in expensive specialist equipment. By using £1, 10p and 1p coins (or their local equivalents if you don't live in the United Kingdom) your child can work out in a practical way how to add and subtract large numbers. This will help him really understand the methods he's using so he's less likely to forget them or use them incorrectly.

There are some other objects your child can count which are even more convenient than coins: his fingers. It's neither cheating nor childish to use them. They're a natural aid to arithmetic which people have used since counting began. The fact that everyone counts on their fingers has even influenced the way numbers have developed: it's not a coincidence that we have ten fingers and we count in tens.

Your child may need your reassurance that it's all right to

count on his fingers, especially if other people have told him that it isn't. Explain that adults do it too sometimes. I know I always do if I have to work out the number of months between August and April.

But surely my child should have stopped needing to count real objects by now?

People vary in how quickly they can switch from counting real objects to working out numbers in their heads. If you make your child stop using coins or fingers before he's ready, you'll just leave him confused and muddled. If you let him go on using them for as long as he wishes, he'll eventually give them up by himself.

Other Equipment

The only equipment you'll need for each session are coins, some gold stars or other rewards, an exercise book and something to write with. A few topics require other items of equipment but these are always either easily available around the house or simply made from paper or card.

In addition, you'll find a calculator useful for setting and marking the questions. Your child will also need to use one for some of the work in Section 3 and may enjoy checking his answers on it at other times. An inexpensive calculator which just adds, subtracts, multiplies and divides is quite good enough.

Should I use a red pen to mark my child's work?

No. Use the same colour pen or pencil as he does. Then you can write in his book while you're working together without your numbers looking very different. The only exception to this is if your child feels it's really important that his work is marked in red (or green or some other colour) but even then you should only use the coloured pen for ticks, not for writing on his work.

Fitting In with School

All children are very conventional and yours is unlikely to be an exception. If your child's teacher has told him to always write the date on the left, he'll be horrified if you suggest he should put it on the right. You'll run into similar problems if you try to use mathematical words, symbols or methods which are different from those used at school.

Look at your child's schoolwork and see whether he uses plain, lined or squared paper for maths. Then make sure he has the same type to use at home with you. Also, wherever possible, use the same words and methods of setting down work as he does at school. If he has an eccentric teacher who always writes questions in green pen, be prepared to do the same if your child thinks it's important.

But surely my child needs to be able to cope with different ways of describing maths?

Yes, of course, he does eventually but it's better not to introduce added complications while he's still trying to grapple with first principles. Also, when you start working together, he'll probably be doubtful about your ability to help. If you confuse him with different words, he may decide your assistance is more trouble than it's worth. Play safe and start the same way as at school.

Oh, dear. It's too late to tell me that now. I've tried helping him in the past and he ended up thoroughly confused and saying his teacher didn't do it like that.

It's never too late to apologize and explain that the confusion was your fault, not his. Tell him you now have this book to help you (let him look at it if he wants) and ask him to help you in future by telling you straight away if you're confusing him or if he doesn't understand.

Organizing Sessions

Keep your maths sessions short. Between ten and twenty minutes is quite long enough as the work is very intensive. If your child needs more help, increase the number of sessions, not their length but don't drive him so hard he becomes sick of maths.

Each session is just for you and your child. Make sure everyone else in your family knows not to interrupt you unless it's absolutely essential. If possible, work away from the distractions of TV and radio and, if someone phones, ask them to call back later.

If you're trying to help more than one child, give each of them separate sessions. Otherwise you won't be able to give them the individual attention they need.

Dividing Up the Time

Each session is divided between oral work (or mental arithmetic) and written work. Always tackle the oral work first as the exercises warm up your child's mind ready for more demanding work to follow. You'll find more detail on organizing this part of the session in chapter 10 and at intervals through the rest of the book.

There are no fixed rules on how long to spend on each part of the session. If you want to spend more time on the oral work, you can set easy written work which can be done quickly. When you want to concentrate on the written work, you can keep the oral session brief.

DON'T FORGET

- **Always have coins available for counting**
- **Never stop your child counting on his fingers**
- **Have all the equipment ready before you start**
- **Fit in with school wherever possible**
- **Always do both oral work and written work in each session**

---

6 / Writing the Exercises

Writing maths exercises for your child is much easier than it sounds. Even if you've never done it before, you should be able to manage without much trouble provided you remember the following advice.

- Always write the exercise before you start the session. It's much easier to think up the questions without your child breathing down your neck.
- Start each exercise with an easy question to build your child's confidence.
- End each exercise with an easy question so she can finish the session with success.
- Use the guidelines for each step to help you make up the questions. If you're not quite sure what to do, go back to the sample exercise to see how those questions fit the guidelines.
- Adjust the length of the exercises to suit the time you have available and the speed at which your child works. If you need to shorten the sample exercises, make sure you keep the easy questions at the beginning and at the end.
- Don't panic if you accidentally write a question which is too hard. Just admit you've made a mistake and change the question to an easier one.

Avoiding Boredom

When your child needs to stay on one level for a long time before she's ready to move on, you must be careful to avoid her becoming bored. One way to do this is to vary the way you write the exercises.

One method I find very successful is to write the questions complete with answers (some right, some wrong) and let your child play teacher and mark them.

$$3 + 9 = 12$$
$$3 + 9 = 11$$

$$6 + 8 = 13$$
$$6 + 8 = 14$$

$$5 + 2 = 8$$
$$5 + 2 = 7$$

You can also try writing the questions down one side of the page and the answers down the other in a different order. Then ask your child to link the correct questions and answers together with arrows.

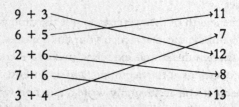

If you wish, you can also occasionally add variety by using exercises from books. Make sure you check each one carefully before you use it to make sure it's at exactly the right level for your child.

If your child stays on one level for a long time, it's often a good idea to leave the topic for a while and come back to it later. Don't on any account move on to the next stage: she's not ready for that. Instead practise some work from previous steps or try another topic from Section 3 for which your child already has the necessary background.

Revision

Learning maths is hard work but forgetting it is remarkably easy. While your child is learning new skills, she also needs occasionally to practise the previous ones to help her remember them. This practice is called revision and it's very important that you include some revision work in the exercises you write for your child.

How you do this is up to you. You may decide to make every third or fourth exercise a revision one or to add one or two revision questions to each exercise. Also, when the work I suggest is designed to fit into the oral work, you can use revision questions for the written part of the session.

One of the values of revision is that your child will find it easier than tackling new topics. This makes it very useful as a break from harder work or to rebuild confidence lost after attempting work which is too difficult. You can also use it to show your child how much she has improved.

DON'T FORGET
- **Write each exercise before you start the session**
- **Start with an easy question**
- **Finish with an easy question**
- **Make the exercises the right length for your child**
- **Revise previous topics regularly**

---

7 / Hints for Helpful Parents

When you were at school I expect you were taught maths by watching your teacher work through questions on the board before you tried to do similar ones yourself. It's almost certainly this 'watch it, then try it' method which has failed with your child so you're not going to use it. Instead of your child watching you, you're going to watch him and, whenever necessary, work with him. To make this easy, you need to sit beside him throughout each session.

When his confidence is very low, you may need to do a great deal of the work while he makes only a small contribution. For example, the first time you ask him to count backwards from twenty, you may need to count with him, saying each number slowly so he can join in.

As he gains in confidence and skill, you can gradually reduce the amount of help you give. For instance, in the case of counting backwards, you can continue to count with him but hesitate a little before each number to give him a chance to say it first. Then you can try letting him count alone but help him out if he hesitates for longer than usual. (In maths a long blank pause is rarely followed by a flash of inspiration.)

You can work together in a similar way on written sums but let him do the actual writing whenever possible. That way it remains *his* work. Leaving aside such complications as broken arms, there are only two occasions when you may need to do some of the writing. One is when you need to show him how to set down his working clearly. The other is if he panics and freezes so he needs help to get him started again. In both cases, you should take over for the minimum possible amount of time.

Preventing Mistakes

Your aim is to make sure your child gets all the written questions right. That doesn't mean he won't make any mistakes. Of course he will. We all do. The art is to make sure that those mistakes don't result in wrong answers.

That's not as hard as it sounds. If you watch your child carefully, you can spot his mistakes as soon as he makes them and give him a chance to put them right, so he still gets the correct answer in the end.

REMEMBER
- **Never tell your child the right answer.**
- **Let him work it out himself (with your help if necessary)**

Be gentle when you point out his mistakes. Avoid negative words like 'wrong' and 'no': he's heard those too many times already. 'Have another look', 'oops' or 'try again' are more encouraging alternatives.

You may prefer not to use words at all. Whenever I'm helping a child, I cough loudly when I spot a mistake: a signal that soon becomes a secret joke between the two of us. There can be a problem if I catch a cold but that usually causes giggles rather than real confusion.

But I'm not very good at maths myself. What happens if I don't spot his mistake until right at the end when I'm actually marking his answers?

Even at that late stage, you can suggest he looks at it again and delay your marking until he's put the answer right.

Discouraging Guessing

Once your child knows he's made a mistake, he's likely to feel flustered and try to guess the answer. He may also guess at other times, especially if he's already got into the habit of doing so at school.

Although guessing may sometimes produce the right answer, it won't help your child to learn so you need to discourage him from doing it. Encourage him to go back to first principles instead and work out the answers he doesn't know. For example, if he's forgotten that $6 + 3 = 9$, let him count on his fingers to find the answer. This will help him remember it next time. Making random guesses won't.

Encouraging Neatness

Untidiness breeds mistakes so always encourage your child to write his maths neatly. Even if he understands hundreds, tens and units, he's unlikely to add large numbers accurately unless he writes them with the figures in the correct columns. Try to set him a good example by always writing his exercises neatly yourself.

DON'T FORGET
- **Watch your child while he works**
- **Give as much help as he needs**
- **Point out mistakes as soon as they happen**
- **Praise success**
- **Discourage guessing**
- **Don't tell him the answers**
- **Encourage neat work**

---

8 / Dealing with Difficulties

It's very frustrating to find that your child doesn't understand something which you have just carefully explained to her. It's tempting to repeat the same explanation again several decibels louder but raising your voice won't help. She'll just think you're getting cross with her (and she may well be right).

Once that happens, it's easy to find yourself in a rapidly deteriorating situation. She becomes tense because she thinks you're angry. That disturbs her concentration, so she starts to make silly mistakes. You become angrier. She starts to panic. You shout even louder. She bursts into tears and you both wish you'd never started working together.

It's not impossible to recover from such a disaster (more of this later) but it's much better to avoid it if you can. The golden rules to follow while helping your child are KEEP CALM and DON'T SHOUT. Both are easier said than done, especially when you're tired or your child seems to have forgotten everything she knew last week. Don't attempt the impossible. We all have good and bad days. If you know you're having a bad one, it's better to skip a session than risk shouting at your child. Similarly, don't try to help your child if she's overtired, ill or thoroughly preoccupied with the arrival of a new gerbil.

If you feel your temper rising during a session, make a deliberate effort to calm down. Breathe slowly and deeply. Relax your body, especially your shoulders. Sip a drink, if you have one available. (If you haven't, you could break the tension by going to make one for you both.) Instead of shouting, attempt to lower your voice. If you speak slowly and gently, you'll feel calmer and so will your child. Then try to put the situation in perspective – you're dealing with one child with a wrong answer, not the outbreak of World War III.

Recognizing Panic

Your child's mistakes don't just upset you. For her, they're yet another sign that she's stupid and that the whole subject is beyond her comprehension. *Beware!* Such thoughts frequently produce panic and panic makes learning impossible.

Think back to a time when you felt very worried yourself. Can you remember how your mind went blank, how you couldn't think properly and your stomach churned? If that's how your child feels, it's hardly surprising she can't do her maths. To help her, you need to spot anxiety early and deal with it before panic takes control. Keep your eyes open for any of the following signs:

- Freezing – a longer pause than usual in work or speech, often accompanied by a blank stare.
- Clenching her hands tightly, perhaps sticking her fingernails into her palms or gripping her pencil hard.
- Biting her nails, chewing her pencil, sucking her thumb or twisting and pulling her hair. (These signs may indicate thought rather than anxiety – use your knowledge of your child to guide you here.)
- Wild guessing at answers: the more intense the anxiety, the wilder the guesses.
- Attempts to change the subject or distract you.
- A sudden request to go to the toilet (not necessarily just an excuse: panic naturally triggers the bladder to empty).
- Tears.
- Anger: yelling, banging the table, throwing the book across the room, etcetera.

Dealing with Panic

When your child is finding the work difficult, it's extra important that she knows you're still on her side. That's one reason why shouting can do so much damage. It puts you firmly on the side of the teachers. Similarly, laughing at her puts you on the side of the children at school who make fun of her mistakes.

However much she panics, stay calm yourself and work with her to finish the task she has started. If some of the questions really are too hard, make sure she realizes this is your fault, not hers. Then either change them to easier ones or miss them out completely. But make sure she still tackles the easy question at the end of the exercise so she finishes the session with success.

You may need to be firm to prevent her giving up but there's no reason why you can't be kind at the same time. As you work together, talk gently with warmth and understanding and reassure her that you're confident she'll learn maths successfully in the end. Hand her some tissues to mop up her tears and, if she throws the book across the room, calmly put it back on the table and carry on. Praise any small sign of success, good behaviour or cooperation and remind her of the reward she's working towards: positive input is much more productive than nagging.

When you first start to help your child, she may panic very easily because she has so little confidence with maths. As her skills improve, she'll become happier with numbers, more confident of her own ability and so less inclined to panic.

DON'T FORGET
- **Keep calm**
- **Don't shout**
- **Try to deal with anxiety before it turns to panic**

---

9 / Games Which Help

Maths isn't just a school subject. Cooking, shopping, gardening and other everyday activities provide excellent opportunities for your child to put his number skills to practical use.

Games can also provide useful maths practice. Although some of those on the market are especially designed as educational aids, there are also many other more traditional ones which involve numbers. Choose ones which are fun to play and which only expect your child to use the number skills he has already acquired.

DON'T FORGET
- **Playing games should be fun**
- **Use games to practise existing skills, not to teach new ones**

Computers and Electronic Games

There's a wide selection of educational software and electronic games which give practice with simple sums. These can be very successful because most children are willing to look at a screen and press keys for far longer than they'll concentrate with a pencil and paper.

Choose carefully if you're planning to invest in such equipment for your child. If possible, try to see the game working before you commit yourself. Failing that, ask the school or other parents for advice or read the reviews in educational and computer magazines. Don't use price as a guide; the best is not necessarily the most expensive. Look out for the following useful features:

- Several levels of difficulty so you can adjust the sums to your child's ability.
- The ability to practise one multiplication table at a time.
- More than one attempt allowed before the correct answer is given. This allows time for rethinking and means that accidentally pressing the wrong key isn't a disaster.

Playing Cards

An ordinary pack of cards can provide a wide variety of different games at minimal cost. You probably know many of them already and you should be able to find books with other ideas in your local library or bookshop. Don't ignore simple games like Snap because they're mathematically undemanding. They can be very helpful if your child panics at the mere sight of numbers.

Many games of Patience involve ordering the numbers (putting them in sequence) forwards or backwards. Whist and other games based on winning tricks require the players to judge which is the largest of a group of numbers.

Pontoon is the best game I've met for practising addition and subtraction of numbers up to twenty-one. Because it contains an element of chance, your child can play happily with the rest of the family without being at a disadvantage because he's less good at maths. If you object to gambling you can leave out that aspect of the game, but playing with matchsticks or other small objects adds more fun and extra counting practice.

Board Games

Any game which involves throwing dice and moving counters will help build confidence with numbers. You can add to the challenge by using two dice and working out the move by adding the two numbers or finding the difference between them. You can also try multiplying the numbers but that whizzes you round the board rather fast.

There's a huge selection of suitable board games on the market with new ones added each year. If you're trying to choose one, don't forget Snakes and Ladders. Its long-lasting popularity is well deserved. The rules are simple and the result is unpredictable because the person in the lead can so easily drop back at any time.

Another long-term favourite is Monopoly which has the extra advantage of using money. Your child needs to be reasonably competent with numbers before he plays it but it can provide excellent practice, especially if he acts as banker. Because you go round and round the board, you can try deciding the move by multiplying the numbers on the dice. It will greatly increase the number of times you pass GO and collect £200.

Keeping Score

Score keeping comes into many games. Mostly this just means adding numbers together but some games are more complicated. Scrabble and darts both involve multiplying by two and three while the darts game 301 gives very good practice at subtraction.

Don't give your child the total responsibility for scoring unless you're sure he can cope. Other players can be less than sympathetic if the scorer makes mistakes. Unless the numbers involved are well within his capabilities, it's better at first to let him assist you.

Pairs

Pairs or Pelmanism can be so useful that it's worth considering on its own. Several matching pairs of cards are mixed up and spread on the floor face down. One player picks up two cards. If they match, the player keeps them. If they don't, he puts them down again exactly where they came from and the next person has a go. The winner is the one with the most pairs at the end of the game.

Provided you use identical pieces of card, it's easy to create your own pairs games to practise specific maths skills. Make the pairs of cards form the two halves of a sum (for example, $2 + 4$ and 6 or 4×3 and 12) or mark them with the same fraction written in different ways (for example, $\frac{1}{4}$ and $\frac{2}{8}$, or $\frac{1}{3}$ and $\frac{2}{6}$).

Summary

1 *Do* praise all success and signs of improvement
2 *Do* keep sessions short
3 *Do* sit with your child all the time he's working and concentrate on what he's doing
4 *Do* start each session with oral counting work
5 *Do* encourage neat work. Neatness improves accuracy especially as maths becomes more complicated
6 *Do* stay on each level of work until he's completely confident
7 *Do* be prepared to drop back to easier work if your child is under stress or loses confidence
8 *Do* let him work at his own speed
9 *Do* let him count on his fingers
10 *Do* make sure your child succeeds
11 *Don't* think you can't help
12 *Don't* introduce competition
13 *Don't* say 'hurry up' – speed will come with increased confidence and competence
14 *Don't* say 'no' or 'wrong'. There are many gentler ways of pointing out mistakes
15 *Don't* mark with a red pen unless your child asks you to

16 *Don't* laugh at your child but do laugh with him
17 *Don't* do maths when your child is sick, overtired or thoroughly preoccupied with a new gerbil
18 *Don't* do maths when you are sick, overtired or thoroughly preoccupied with the leaky plumbing
19 *Don't* shout or lose your temper
20 *Don't* forget to praise every sign of progress

10 / Starting the Oral Work

Maths is a thinking activity. The old-fashioned division between ordinary sums and mental arithmetic is an artificial one. In reality we do all our work with numbers in our heads even if we sometimes use counters, fingers or pencil and paper to help us. That's why it's so vital that we have a mental image of numbers and the way they relate to each other. We can show this relationship by writing the numbers along a line in the same way as they would appear on a ruler or tape measure.

0 1 2 3 4 5 6 7 8 9 10 11 12

Teachers call this type of picture a number line. Sometimes they use a vertical line instead and write the numbers as they would appear on a thermometer.

Your child may be used to using a number line at school to help her with her maths, so provide both types at home in case she wants to use them. They don't have to be very elaborate. Just copy each of the number lines on to separate pieces of paper or thin card.

12
11
10
9
8
7
6
5
4
3
2
1
0

Let's Start at the Very Beginning

Before your child can learn addition, subtraction, multiplication and division, she must be able to count accurately. That's why she spent so long practising this skill when she started school.

Check It Out

Before you start any formal maths sessions, check whether your child can count small numbers of objects confidently and competently. Can she, for example,

- fetch three onions while you are cooking,
- put four plates on the table,
- tell you how many eggs are left in the box?

If she can do this type of task, she understands the basic concept of counting, so it's safe to move on to other tasks.

If she can't cope with these tasks, don't start formal maths sessions yet: the risk of failure is too high. Instead use the time for counting practice. As well as involving your child in any counting which occurs naturally during cooking, shopping and other activities, you could try:

- Letting her count different numbers of chocolate buttons and then eat them.
- Playing Snakes and Ladders and other board games involving throwing dice and moving counters.
- Playing any card game which starts with each player having a set number of cards and letting your child be the dealer.
- Playing any card game which involves players paying penalties by laying down or picking up two, three or more cards at a time.

During all these activities, count with your child until she gets the idea, then gradually let her take over and do it on her own. Be prepared to help again if she gets stuck.

***When my child learnt to count at school, her teacher kept
talking about sets. What are they and are they important?***

A set is just what you would guess it to be: a collection of
objects. When your child's counting a pile of sweets, you
could say instead that she's counting a set of sweets. If her
teacher has used 'set' in this way, your child may use the word
too but it won't matter if you don't. It also doesn't matter if
your child has never met the idea of sets. Although she'll need
to know about them if she decides to be a mathematician, she
doesn't need to know about them now.

Starting to Work Together

Once you're sure your child can count objects, you're ready to
start your first proper maths session together. This session is a
very important one for the success of the whole system. Despite
all your efforts to gain her cooperation, your child will probably
still be plagued with doubts. Do you know what you're doing?
Is it worth making this extra effort when she already knows she's
useless? Will you lose your temper if she fails? You probably
have a few doubts of your own too, so this first session isn't
just about helping with maths. It's about building confidence.

The oral work you're going to do is based on counting.
Your child can already count forwards (one, two, three . . .).
Now you're going to help her build her mental picture of
numbers by asking her to count in other ways (backwards, for
example). As memory alone can't provide the answers, she'll
be forced to think hard about the way the numbers relate to
each other and this will improve both her mental agility and
her understanding.

At first, your child may find these other ways of counting
very difficult and will need a great deal of help. However,
she'll improve rapidly and this may be the first concrete sign
she sees that your work together is having effect.

Tackling the First Session

Before you start, make sure you've everything ready and write the first exercise from the next chapter into your child's book. Then ask your child to sit beside you.

Step 1
Once you're both settled, remind her that you're going right back to the beginning of maths and ask her to count to ten. She'll manage this without any trouble.

Say something like 'Good. Now we've proved you can do maths. All we've got to do now is help you learn the parts you haven't got the hang of yet.'

Step 2
Now ask her to count to twenty. She'll probably manage this all right. If she makes a mistake or hesitates, you've started to find where her problems lie. Gently point out the mistake and give her a chance to correct it herself. If she hesitates for a long time, help her out by saying the correct answer.

When she reaches twenty, say 'good' or 'well done'. Give similar acknowledgements of success whenever she completes an activity.

REMEMBER
Mistakes damage self-confidence. It's important not to seem critical or threatening when you point them out, so avoid saying 'no' or 'that's wrong'. It is better to say 'oops', 'have another go' or just cough gently. If she seems upset, remind her that everyone makes mistakes sometimes, even you.

Step 3
The next step is to ask her to count backwards from ten. If she's very unsure of herself, count with her. Speak slowly

enough to give her a chance to say the numbers first if she can but not so slowly that there are huge gaps if she's stuck. Don't forget to praise her when she's finished.

If your child found counting to twenty very difficult, leave out step 4 and go straight on to the written work.

If your child could count to twenty with little or no help, continue to step 4.

Step 4

The last stage of this first oral session is to ask your child to count backwards in ones from twenty to zero. She's likely to find this more difficult than step 3 as she's probably spent less time at school working with the teen numbers than she has with those from one to ten.

Don't worry if she counts very slowly because she has to keep working out the next number. Let her take her time: the thought processes she's carrying out are very beneficial. Reassure her that speed doesn't matter and praise her progress as she works.

REMEMBER
- If she makes a mistake, point it out gently
- If she gets stuck, help her out with the next number
- If she lacks confidence, count with her

When she's finished these four steps, move on to the written work described in the next chapter.

If she doesn't do one of the counting exercises very well, should I ask her to try it again?

Only if you think she's likely to improve the second time. There's no point in reinforcing failure. If she was hesitant but fairly successful, you can say something like 'That's coming on well. Have another go and see if you can do it even better.'

Don't ask her to repeat anything more than once. Boredom sets in easily and there will be plenty of chance for more practice in future sessions.

Does it matter if she uses her fingers as she counts?

Let her use them if they help her. She'll stop using them of her own accord when she feels ready. It's also all right for her to count coins or other objects.

Is it all right to let her use a number line?

Yes. All you're concentrating on in this session is getting her to succeed and building her confidence, so let her use anything which helps. In later sessions, you can encourage her to cover it up and only peep when she gets stuck. That way she'll think about the numbers rather than just reading them.

Organizing Further Oral Work

Your subsequent oral sessions will work in much the same way as this first one but you can gradually extend the work as your child gains confidence and competence. You'll find ideas for doing this in the rest of this chapter and at intervals throughout the book. I also occasionally suggest oral work to tie in with the topic your child is learning.

Remember always to start each session with some easy counting work. This'll wake your child up mentally in much the same way that an athlete's gentle stretching exercises warm her up physically.

Developing Counting

Because the pattern repeats all the time, counting doesn't become progressively harder as the numbers increase in size. So once your child can count to twenty easily, try counting forwards from twenty to forty, from seventy to ninety, etcetera. Also when she can count backwards from twenty absolutely confidently, try counting backwards from forty to thirty, from eighty to sixty, etcetera.

There's no need to restrict yourself to numbers less than a hundred. Occasionally counting very large numbers can boost confidence. How about trying going from one million to one million and twenty?

Solving Simple Sums

The easiest sums build on the fact that the processes of counting forwards and adding one are the same. Ask questions such as 'Which number is one larger than seven?' or 'Which number is one more than twelve?'

In the same way, counting backwards is the same process as taking away one. Once your child can count backwards fairly happily, try asking questions like 'Which number is one smaller than three?' or 'Which number is one less than fourteen?'

As she progresses to counting larger numbers, you can introduce these into the questions. For instance, you could ask 'Which number is one more than eighty-four?' or 'Which number is one smaller than sixty-three?'

Don't ask her to add or take away a number greater than one until she has tackled this in the written work.

BE CAREFUL
Don't ask your child which number comes before or after another one. The answer depends on whether you are counting forwards or backwards.

Counting in Patterns

Once your child can count forward happily, you can introduce the idea of counting in patterns. Start with counting in twos. You need only go as far as twenty at the moment. Starting at zero or two gives you the even numbers. Starting at one gives you the odd ones.

Initially your child may need to count all the numbers but only say every other one out loud like this: 'One . . . *two* . . . three . . . *four* . . . five . . . *six* . . . seven . . . *eight* . . .' She may prefer you to say the alternate numbers instead of whispering them herself. You can throw a ball between you at the same time if you like.

With practice, she'll gain confidence and remember the pattern so she can count quickly in twos and easily continue beyond twenty to a hundred. At this stage, you can reinforce the skill by getting her to count backwards in twos from twenty.

Once she can count confidently in twos, you can introduce other number patterns. Ten and five are the simplest so they build confidence before you tackle three, four, six, eight, nine and seven. Don't rush. It's better to concentrate on one or two patterns until your child knows them well rather than to jump about from one to the other so she never remembers anything.

DON'T FORGET
- **Keep oral sessions short**
- **Start each session with easy work**
- **Praise success**
- **Give help whenever it's needed**
- *Don't rush* **– only make the work harder very gradually**

---

11 / Basic Addition

Addition is straightforward and is usually taught well at school so I'm sure your child will understand the basic concept. However he may still be only part way along the learning path which leads to being able to add numbers quickly and accurately.

Imagine you've asked him this question: 'You've got three pennies and I have two. How many pennies have we got altogether?'

He may tackle this in one of three ways:

1) He may count out three coins or fingers and two coins or fingers and then count how many he has – 'one, two, three, four, five'.
2) He may count on to find the answer. That means he starts from the first number (three) and counts on another two by saying 'four, five'. Similarly to work out 2 + 4, he starts from two and counts on four, saying 'three, four, five, six' He'll probably use his fingers, coins, dots or a number line to help him to count.
3) He may know the answer is five because he can remember it from past experience.

These different methods illustrate the three stages all children go through to master the process of adding numbers together. Some of them get stuck at stage 1 and need to be shown how to count on. Some need to be encouraged to move from counting coins or dots to using their more readily available fingers.

If your child cannot yet answer the questions from memory

(as in stage 3), there's no point in trying to force him to do so. Only practice will help him remember the answers and it's perfectly natural for his progress to be patchy. For example, he may easily remember $5 + 4 = 9$ but keep forgetting $2 + 4 = 6$.

REMEMBER
Never, ever, tell your child not to use his fingers for counting. They're a natural aid to arithmetic and there's nothing wrong with using them. He'll stop using them of his own accord when he feels ready.

What are number bonds? My child's teacher keeps saying he should learn them but I don't know what she means.

Number bonds is educational jargon for the simple facts which connect numbers together. $2 + 2 = 4$ is a number bond. So are $3 + 4 = 7$, $8 + 1 = 9$ and all the other similar addition questions your child will tackle in this chapter. When his teacher says she wants your child to learn his number bonds, she means she wants him to be able to answer these questions from memory. Don't let the jargon frighten you: you're both aiming at the same goal.

Step 1

Aims:
1) To show your child he can succeed at maths.
2) To check which method your child uses to add numbers together.
3) To find the best length of exercise for your child.

Equipment
In addition to your standard equipment (see chapter 5), have a horizontal and a vertical number line available in case your child wants to use one.

Before You Start the Session
Write the date on the first page of your child's book. Then write these questions down the left-hand side of the page.

1)	$2 + 3 =$	6)	$3 + 5 =$
2)	$4 + 1 =$	7)	$3 + 4 =$
3)	$5 + 2 =$	8)	$1 + 2 =$
4)	$1 + 3 =$	9)	$2 + 4 =$
5)	$4 + 4 =$	10)	$3 + 3 =$

To write more exercises, make up questions which involve adding two numbers together. Make both numbers five or less so that your child won't run out of fingers if he wants to use them to find the answers.

Tackling the Exercise
Show your child these questions after you've finished the oral part of the session. Watch his reactions carefully: they'll show you what help he needs.

REMEMBER
You can't help him properly unless you can see what he's doing.
If he curls his arm around his book to hide his work, ask him to move it out of the way.

If he can answer the questions easily, he may argue that they're too easy and won't help him with his schoolwork. If so, remind him again why you've gone back to the beginning of maths (see chapter 4). Tell him how pleased you are that he can already do these sums and assure him that the work will quite quickly become more challenging.

If he seems worried by the questions and hesitates to start, try to demystify the first question by reading it aloud without using mathematical words like add and plus. For example, you could say 'If there are two dolphins and three more arrive, how many are there altogether?' (You can replace dolphins

with other things your child likes – ponies, spaceships, football-
ers, cream buns, etcetera.)

If he still hesitates or tries unsuccessfully to guess the answer,
suggest that he might like to use his fingers or some pennies to
help him. Also show him the number lines and say he's
welcome to use one if he does at school. (Don't confuse the
issue by trying to teach him to use it now.)

Don't worry if he draws dots on the page to represent the
numbers and then counts them. This isn't wrong: it's just a
variation on using coins. Let him do it if he feels happier that
way but make it clear that he's welcome to use the coins or his
fingers if he wishes.

If he still looks hesitant and worried despite your reassurances,
work the first question with him by counting pennies. Praise
him when he gets the right answer. Continue through the
other questions, letting him take over and do them by himself
if and when he wants to.

Offering Encouragement

As he finishes each question, he may look at you to see how
he's doing. Reassure him that he has the right answer by
nodding, giving a thumbs up sign or saying 'good'.

Remember to point out any mistakes as soon as they happen.
(Don't wait until the end of the exercise.) When he has sorted
out his mistake, let him cross out the wrong answer and
correct it. Then, when you're sure he has answered all the
questions successfully, you can tick them and tell him how
pleased you are.

Moving On

What you do next depends on how your child has coped with
the work so far.

a) If he's really struggled to answer the questions using the
   basic counting method or counting on and has needed a lot

of help, he's done enough for today. Give him a gold star or other reward and end the session.

He needs to stay at this level until he finds the work easier. Follow the instructions earlier in this step to make up suitable exercises for your next sessions. Don't worry if you repeat questions from previous exercises. This is unavoidable and the repetition will help him learn the answers.

When he can answer the questions confidently by himself with only occasional mistakes, move on to step 2 in your next session.

b) If he's answered the questions by counting or counting on with only a little help, he can already cope with work at this level. If he doesn't want to continue or you've no time left, give him a star and end the session. Move on to step 2 for your next session.

If you still have some time left and he wants to continue, write all or some of these sums (depending on the time available) down the centre of the same page. They're the same level as the original ones.

11)	$5 + 1 =$	16)	$1 + 5 =$
12)	$2 + 2 =$	17)	$3 + 2 =$
13)	$5 + 5 =$	18)	$5 + 3 =$
14)	$1 + 1 =$	19)	$2 + 1 =$
15)	$4 + 5 =$	20)	$1 + 4 =$

When he's finished these, mark them, praise his success and give him a star. Then move on to step 2 in your next session.

c) If your child answered all the questions easily from memory, tell him that you're so impressed with his maths that he's ready to go straight on to the next stage. Write these questions down the centre of the same page. They include some at the same level as the ones in step 2.

11)	6 + 3 =	16)	3 + 7 =
12)	3 + 5 =	17)	4 + 5 =
13)	4 + 6 =	18)	9 + 1 =
14)	2 + 7 =	19)	8 + 2 =
15)	6 + 2 =	20)	5 + 5 =

If he answers these easily from memory, move on to step 3 for your next session.

If he makes several mistakes or needs to use counting on to find the answers, move on to step 2 for your next session.

Step 2

Aims:
1) To give further practice at addition.
2) To introduce the idea of counting on if your child doesn't already use it.

Before You Start the Session
Write this exercise in your child's book. If necessary, adjust the length to suit the speed at which your child works.

1)	3 + 6 =	11)	4 + 6 =
2)	4 + 2 =	12)	3 + 7 =
3)	2 + 5 =	13)	7 + 2 =
4)	4 + 5 =	14)	4 + 3 =
5)	5 + 3 =	15)	6 + 2 =
6)	5 + 5 =	16)	1 + 9 =
7)	6 + 3 =	17)	3 + 5 =
8)	4 + 4 =	18)	3 + 4 =
9)	2 + 7 =	19)	2 + 2 =
10)	8 + 2 =	20)	8 + 1 =

To write more exercises, use the numbers from one to nine to make up similar questions whose answers are all no larger than ten. This will make sure that your child can count on his fingers to work out the answer, although he won't always be able to show each number on a separate hand.

Tackling the Exercise

Show your child these questions when you've finished the oral part of the session. If he already uses counting on to work out the answers, let him work through the exercise at his own speed, offering help if he needs it.

If he doesn't yet use counting on, let him answer the first four questions in his usual way to help build his confidence. When he reaches question 5, wait until he's counted out a group of five fingers (or coins) and a group of three fingers. As he starts to count them all, you can encourage him to count on instead. Your conversation might sound like this:

YOU: You don't really need to count that first group. You've already done that. How many are there?

CHILD: Five

YOU: That's right. So you can just pretend you've counted them and then count the others. Go on.

CHILD: (*misunderstanding*): One, two, three.

YOU: Yes, there's three there but we need to find how many there are altogether. Imagine we've counted the first five and we're going to count on from there. I'll do it with you.

TOGETHER: Six, seven, eight.

YOU: Good. That's right. If you like, you can check that's right by counting them all.

CHILD: One, two, three, four, five, six, seven, eight.

YOU: You see, it's the same answer. Now write that down and we'll try the next one the same way.

Continue to encourage your child to use counting on for the rest of the exercise, giving as much or as little help as he needs. Don't be surprised if he doesn't greet your suggestion with delight. He's used to his own method which works and may be wary of this newfangled idea. He may need a great deal of encouragement to keep trying this new method until he gets used to it. He may also need to work a number of sums both ways before he's convinced that it works.

Moving On
Stay on this level until your child can answer the questions confidently using counting on with only occasional help to avoid mistakes. Then move on to step 3 in your next session.

Step 3

Aims:
1) To practise addition with larger answers.
2) To provide enough practice for your child to start to
   remember some of the answers.

Before You Start the Session
Write this exercise in your child's book:

1)	3 + 4 =	11)	7 + 6 =
2)	2 + 5 =	12)	8 + 9 =
3)	6 + 5 =	13)	7 + 3 =
4)	8 + 3 =	14)	0 + 7 =
5)	4 + 9 =	15)	2 + 7 =
6)	6 + 6 =	16)	7 + 7 =
7)	8 + 0 =	17)	6 + 3 =
8)	2 + 9 =	18)	7 + 4 =
9)	9 + 7 =	19)	9 + 1 =
10)	8 + 8 =	20)	8 + 2 =

To write more exercises, make up similar addition questions using any of the numbers from zero to nine. Try to include all the possible pairs of numbers. Don't worry if you repeat questions you've already asked in previous exercises. The repetition will help your child to remember the answers.

Unless your child can already answer these questions from memory, he'll need to stay on this level for quite a few sessions. You can avoid boredom by varying the way you write the exercises (see chapter 6).

You can also ask your child pairs of questions where the second is the reverse of the first (for examples $5 + 8 =$ and $8 + 5 =$). Then help him to spot that, with addition, the answer is always the same whichever order you write the numbers.

Tackling the Exercise
These questions don't require any new skills but your child may be worried at first because some of the answers are larger than ten. This anxiety should soon clear once he finds he can cope with the work.

Adding Zero
When your child reaches question 7, he may make the common mistake of saying $8 + 0 = 0$. If he finds it hard to believe that this is wrong, use coins to illustrate the question. Your conversation might sound like this:

YOU: Suppose I give you eight pennies on Monday. (*Give your child the coins*.) How many have you got?
CHILD: Eight.
YOU: Right. Now on Tuesday I don't give you any more pennies. How many have you got now?
CHILD: Eight.

You can repeat this explanation using other numbers until your child believes you.

BY THE WAY
It doesn't matter whether you call 0 nought or zero but never, ever, call it oh. That's the name of the letter not the number.

Why is it that one day he seems to know most of the answers straight away, but the next time he needs to work them all out?

This is normal. Everyone has good and bad days and your child is no exception. Although it's frustrating to watch, try to resist the temptation to yell at him or make a fuss about it. As his knowledge and his confidence grow with practice, he'll forget less often.

Moving On

Stay on this level until your child can remember at least some of the answers and can work out the others using counting on with only occasional help to avoid mistakes. Then move on to step 1 of subtraction. Don't worry that there are still answers he can't remember. He'll learn those as he works through the rest of this section.

DEVELOPING THE ORAL WORK   1

You've already started asking your child questions like 'Which number is one larger than four?' As soon as he can confidently add numbers by counting on, you can also include questions like 'Which number is two more than three?' or 'Which number is two greater than seven?'

When he can add two easily, move on to adding three, then four, etcetera.

Varying the Words

You can also start to introduce number stories which will help your child become accustomed to the many different ways of describing maths. For instance, 'Which number is one more than three?' could become: 'Honey, the cat, had three kittens. Matilda, the cat next door, had kittens too but she had one more than Honey. How many kittens did Matilda have?'

At first your child may find it difficult to see the maths hidden in the words, so keep the actual addition very simple. Then he'll have the satisfaction of being able to answer the question easily once he realizes what he has to do.

Counting in Patterns
In chapter 13 your child will start to work with numbers greater than twenty. To understand this work easily, he must be able to count in tens so make sure he practises this skill during the oral part of your sessions as you work through chapter 12. When he can confidently count in tens, you can also introduce counting in hundreds.

12 / Basic Subtraction

Subtraction is the opposite process to addition. That might sound complicated but it just means that if you add a number and then take away the same number, you return to where you started.

What is Subtraction?

Look at these questions:

- If I have nine and take away six, how many are left?
- How many less than nine is six?
- How many more than six is nine?

Although only one of them talks about taking away, they're all subtraction questions. In fact they're the same one: $9 - 6 = 3$.

These three different ways of wording the same question lead naturally to the three most common methods of tackling subtraction: taking away, counting on and counting back.

Taking Away

This is probably the way your child first met subtraction at school. To tackle the question 'If I have nine and take away six, how many are left?', she'll count out nine coins or fingers, take away six of them and count how many are left.

Counting how many are left each time she folds down a finger or takes away a coin leads naturally to working out the answer by counting back six places from nine (eight, seven, six, five, four, three). She'll probably continue to use her fingers to help her or she may be used to counting back along a number line.

This method is very useful for subtracting small numbers but is less suitable for subtracting large ones.

Counting On

Counting on arises naturally from the question 'How much bigger is nine than six?' If your child has a line of six coins, she has to add extra coins until there are nine. As she lays the coins down, she counts seven, eight, nine. Then she counts how many coins she has laid down to find that the answer is three.

Eventually she won't bother to count the original six, but will just count on from six to nine. As she counts, she'll probably match each number against a coin or (more likely) a finger so she can easily see the final answer. This method adapts easily to large numbers. For instance, she could work out 69 − 64, by counting on from sixty-four (sixty-five, sixty-six, sixty-seven, sixty-eight, sixty-nine) to find that the answer is five.

Counting Back

Counting back comes from thinking about 9 − 6 as 'How much smaller is six than nine?' This time your child starts with nine coins or fingers and takes away one at a time until there are six left. As she takes away each one, she says how many are left (eight, seven, six): in effect she counts backwards from nine until she reaches six. The number of coins she has taken away tells her the answer.

Eventually she doesn't need to see the original nine, but can just count backwards matching each number against a finger so that she can easily see the final answer. This technique works well for larger numbers too. For instance, she could work out $79 - 75$ by counting seventy-eight, seventy-seven, seventy-six, seventy-five and seeing that the answer is four.

Which Method?

All three methods are correct so it doesn't matter which one your child uses provided she does so successfully. However, if she's having trouble with subtraction, I suggest that you encourage her to use counting on. This is because, in my experience, people who find maths difficult are happier counting forwards than counting backwards.

Step 1

Aim
To find which method your child uses to subtract.

Before You Start the Session
Write this exercise in your child's book:

1)	$2 - 1 =$		6)	$7 - 2 =$
2)	$3 - 1 =$		7)	$7 - 4 =$
3)	$5 - 2 =$		8)	$8 - 8 =$
4)	$6 - 3 =$		9)	$6 - 2 =$
5)	$4 - 4 =$		10)	$9 - 7 =$

11)	6 − 5 =		16)	7 − 5 =
12)	5 − 3 =		17)	7 − 3 =
13)	8 − 4 =		18)	10 − 3 =
14)	9 − 6 =		19)	9 − 1 =
15)	10 − 5 =		20)	3 − 2 =

To write more exercises, make up similar subtraction questions using numbers no larger than ten. Make sure the second number is always smaller than the first or equal to it. (This is not the right moment to introduce negative numbers.)

Tackling the Exercise
Show your child the questions when you've finished the oral work and encourage her to notice that the signs are different this time. Ask her if she knows what the new sign means? What does her teacher call this type of question? Her answers will show you which words to use yourself.

BE PREPARED
If subtraction has caused her trouble in the past, these questions may reawaken her 'I can't do maths' feelings. Be ready to give plenty of encouragement and praise during this chapter to boost her confidence.

If she seems unsure how to start, turn the first question into words without using the mathematical jargon of minus or subtract. For example, you could say 'If you've got two bars of chocolate and you eat one, how many have you got left?' Repeat this process for each question until she can manage without it.

Once she starts the exercise, she may answer some or all of the questions from memory. When she can't remember the answer, she'll need to work it out. Watch carefully to see which method she uses. You may need to ask her to work aloud instead of in her head so you can follow what she's doing.

Let's consider what may happen when she tackles 5 − 2:

a) She may count out five coins or fingers, take away two and count how many are left. Alternatively she may lay out a line of five coins and a line of two coins and count how many more coins there are in one line than the other. This shows she's still in the early stages of learning subtraction.

b) She may successfully count backwards from five or forwards from two to find the answer. It doesn't matter which method she uses provided she does it correctly. (Don't worry about occasional careless mistakes.) Don't try to force her to change methods just because she uses a different one from you.

c) She may try to count forwards or backwards but start to count in the wrong place. If she's counting forwards from two, the first number she should say is three (not two), just as it would be if she were working out an addition question. If she's counting backwards from five, the first number she should say is four (not five).

Each time she starts to count in the wrong place, gently point out her mistake and encourage her to start again. Count with her, pointing at her fingers as you do so. Let her see that you point at the first finger as you say the number you get when you add or take away one, at the second finger when you say the number which you get when you add or take away two, etcetera. Don't panic if she still doesn't understand. We'll sort out this problem in the next few sessions.

Moving On

1) If your child answered all the questions easily from memory or worked them out correctly by counting forwards or backwards, move on to step 4.

2) If your child still uses the basic method with fingers or counters, move on to step 2.

3) If your child initially made many mistakes when counting backwards or forwards to find the answer but improved with your help, stay on this level for two more exercises. Then:
   - If she still makes many mistakes, move on to step 2.
   - If she only makes occasional slips, move on to step 4.

4) If your child made many mistakes when trying to find the answer by counting forwards or backwards and did not improve very much with your help, move on to step 2.

Step 2

Aim:
To teach your child to use counting on to find the difference between two numbers.

Before You Start the Session
Write this exercise in your child's book:

1)	2 +	= 3		11)	4 +	= 9
2)	2 +	= 5		12)	2 +	= 9
3)	4 +	= 6		13)	5 +	= 8
4)	2 +	= 7		14)	6 +	= 10
5)	6 +	= 8		15)	4 +	= 7
6)	5 +	= 9		16)	3 +	= 5
7)	6 +	= 10		17)	7 +	= 10
8)	4 +	= 8		18)	5 +	= 8
9)	3 +	= 9		19)	6 +	= 7
10)	2 +	= 6		20)	4 +	= 5

To write more exercises, make up addition questions with the second number missed out and the answer written in. Make sure the first number and the answer are no larger than ten.

REMEMBER
Feel free to adjust the length of the sample exercises to suit your child.

Tackling the Exercise

When you show your child the exercise, explain that you want her to write a number in each space to make the sum correct. If she looks blank or hesitates, try turning question 1 into words: 'What number must you add to two to make three?' Because of the work you've already done together, she'll probably be able to tell you the answer from memory.

When she starts the second question, make a picture of the question with coins even if she knows the answer anyway. Put two coins next to each other in a line with five more coins in a line below them. (She may need reassurance that this isn't babyish: it's just to help you explain something.)

Ask her how many coins she needs to add to the top row to make it the same length as the bottom one. She may be able to tell you the answer straight away or she may have to count them. Either way, add the remaining three coins to the top line counting three, four, five as you do so.

Repeat this method for each question. Let her put down the lines of coins herself until she's gained confidence and can do this easily. This may take more than one session.

REMEMBER
Don't rush. You're not in a race. Only move forward at the speed your child learns, even if that seems so slow you could scream.

When you're sure she's ready to move on, ask her to try leaving out the second row in the next question. Let's take 4 + = 6 as an example. Tell her to lay down a line of four coins, leave a small gap and then lay down more coins until the row is six long. Count 'five, six' as she does so. Then let her see how many coins she added (the gap will help her tell where they begin).

Once she can do that confidently, you can suggest that there's really no need to lay out the first line of coins. She can count on from the first number even if she can't see it, just as she does when she's adding. When she can do that successfully, you can gradually encourage her to move from counting coins (which she might not always have with her) to counting her fingers.

Moving On
Stay on this level until your child can answer the questions confidently by counting on from the first number, with or without using coins or fingers. Then move on to step 3.

Step 3

Aim:
To use counting on to answer conventional subtraction questions.

Before You Start
Write this exercise in your child's book:

1)	5 − 3 =	6)	6 − 3 =
2)	4 − 2 =	7)	8 − 5 =
3)	7 − 3 =	8)	6 − 6 =
4)	9 − 6 =	9)	9 − 4 =
5)	6 − 4 =	10)	8 − 3 =

11) $8 - 6 =$ 16) $6 - 1 =$
12) $9 - 7 =$ 17) $7 - 7 =$
13) $5 - 2 =$ 18) $6 - 2 =$
14) $7 - 4 =$ 19) $9 - 8 =$
15) $8 - 3 =$ 20) $5 - 4 =$

To write more exercises, make up subtraction questions with both numbers no larger than ten. The second number should always be smaller than or equal to the first one.

Tackling the Exercise

Before your child starts work, make sure she's realized they're subtraction questions. Otherwise she may add them by mistake.

If she uses counting on successfully without any encouragement from you, tell her how pleased you are and let her continue.

If she goes back to the method she was using before or just looks blank, point out that the first question doesn't just mean 'What's five take away three?' It also means 'What's the difference between three and five?' or 'What do you have to add to three to make five?' Once she realizes that these questions are the same type as in the previous exercise but written differently, you can suggest that she could find the answer to these by counting on. She may accept this idea quite happily. If not, encourage her to try using counting on first and then check her answers using her old method. Once she believes counting on works, she won't need to check each time.

Moving On

Stay on this level until your child can use counting on successfully with only occasional mistakes. Then move on to step 4.

Step 4

Aim
To practise all the subtraction questions which correspond to the addition ones in chapter 11.

Before You Start the Session
Write this exercise in your child's book:

1)	$5 - 3 =$	11)	$15 - 8 =$
2)	$10 - 6 =$	12)	$18 - 9 =$
3)	$9 - 4 =$	13)	$12 - 7 =$
4)	$12 - 3 =$	14)	$13 - 8 =$
5)	$15 - 8 =$	15)	$15 - 6 =$
6)	$11 - 4 =$	16)	$14 - 6 =$
7)	$13 - 5 =$	17)	$9 - 9 =$
8)	$11 - 7 =$	18)	$7 - 6 =$
9)	$16 - 8 =$	19)	$8 - 2 =$
10)	$14 - 9 =$	20)	$6 - 1 =$

To write more exercises, make up subtraction questions where the first number is less than twenty and the second number is less than ten. Make sure the second number is always smaller than or equal to the first one.

Tackling the Exercise
These questions don't require any new skills but your child may be worried because some of the numbers are larger than ten. If necessary, work with her until she feels more confident.

Moving On
Stay on this level until your child can work out all the answers confidently with only occasional mistakes and can remember some of the answers. Then move on to chapter 13.

DEVELOPING THE ORAL WORK 2

Your oral sessions together have already included questions like 'Which number is one smaller than six?' and 'Which number is one less than eight?'

Once your child can subtract confidently, you can gradually extend this part of your work to include similar questions which involve subtracting two. When she can happily cope with these, you can move on to subtracting three, then four, etcetera. You can also vary the wording of the questions to include:

- What must I add to three to make five?
- How much bigger is eight than six?
- What is the difference between four and six?

Using Number Stories

You can now introduce subtraction into your number stories. For example, $5 - 1$ could become 'Five dragons are flying through a clear blue sky. One of them vanishes in a puff of smoke. How many are left?'

Don't forget to keep the actual subtraction very easy so that your child can concentrate on finding the maths question hidden in the words.

Using Larger Numbers

Once your child can confidently count past twenty, you can introduce larger numbers into your oral addition and subtraction work. Try asking her questions like 'Which number is two larger than eighty-six?' to encourage her to count forwards to find the answer and others like 'Which number is two smaller than thirty-five?' to encourage her to count backwards.

Once she can answer these easily, you can gradually move on to adding and subtracting three, then four and so on but don't make the questions too difficult too soon. Remember that 76 − 4 is much easier to work out in your head than 72 − 4.

Counting in Patterns

As you work through chapters 13 and 14, try regularly to include counting in twos and counting in fives in your oral sessions. This will help your child to cope with the work on multiplication in chapter 15.

13 / Place Value or Hundreds, Tens and Units

This chapter is about place value: the fact that the value of a numeral varies according to where it's written. For example, in the number 32 the 2 stands for two ones, in 324 it stands for two tens while in 235 it stands for two hundreds. When you were at school, you may have called this topic hundreds, tens and units and written the initials HTU above each of your sums. Don't worry. It's only the name that has changed, not the maths.

Some of the work in this chapter may look trivially easy but don't be tempted to move on before your child's ready. It's vitally important that he understands place value thoroughly or he'll have trouble working with larger numbers.

WHAT'S IN A NAME?

I find children understand me better if I talk about tens and ones rather than tens and units so I've avoided the word units in this book. However, feel free to change this if your child's already used to talking about units at school and would prefer that you did the same.

Why Do We Count in Tens?

Thousands of years ago man stood upright and took to living in caves and hunting. Counting wasn't a problem. If anyone asked the returning hunter how successful he'd been, he could just show one finger for each animal he'd caught. As most of the animals ran faster than him, there was little chance of him running out of fingers.

Once he settled down to farming, running fast was less important but counting became vital. How else would he know if he still had all his sheep? With a small flock he had no problem; he could still just match each sheep with a finger. But sheep breed and soon he had to count higher than ten. When he'd used up all his fingers, he made a mark on a stick or the ground to show he'd counted two full hands and then started matching his fingers to the remaining sheep. Gradually that simple system developed into the way we count today.

So it's not just coincidence that we count in tens and have ten fingers. It's the most sensible method of counting to use if we're to gain the maximum advantage from our inbuilt aids to arithmetic. If we were all born with six fingers, we would count in a system based on sixes instead.

When my eldest child was at school he had to learn about numbers in different bases. What did that mean and why isn't my youngest child learning it too?

Because our counting system is based on ten, mathematicians say we count in base ten. If we counted in a system based on six, they would say we counted in base six.

Several years ago, the experts decided that it would help children understand our number system if they also tried using different ones. In particular, they thought children should be able to count in the system based on two (base two) because that was the system used by computers which were just becoming popular.

That idea has now gone out of fashion which explains why your youngest child isn't expected to tackle it. Although computers still count in base two in the inner depths of their workings, there's no need for us to understand it before we use a word processor or play Sonic the Hedgehog. More importantly, many teachers have found, as I did, that children having trouble with base 10 weren't helped at all by studying different number systems. They just became more confused.

Equipment

For this chapter, you will need at least ninety pennies, twenty-five 10p pieces and two £1 coins.

You'll also need sixteen pieces of paper or card: six about 4 cm × 6 cm, another six 8 cm × 6 cm and the last four 12 cm × 6 cm. Keep two each of the small and medium size pieces as spares and write numbers on the others as shown in the diagram.

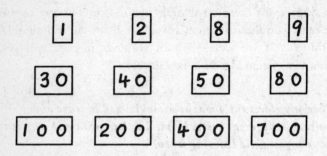

When you've finished, you should be able to put the 50 on top of the 700 and the 1 on top of the 50 so that together they look 751.

Step 1

Aim

To discover how well your child understands place value.

Before You Start the Session

The work in this step is designed to fit into the oral part of your session so you can use the written part for extra practice with basic addition and subtraction. Before you sit down together:

- Write a suitable exercise in your child's book.
- Arrange your cards on the table in groups of three so the numbers which show read as 131, 452, 789 and 248.

Tackling the Oral Work

Start the session with one or two straightforward counting exercises. Then point out the cards and ask your child to read you the four numbers. If he says one three one, explain that, although people sometimes say numbers that way, you'd like him to say them in the more usual way: one hundred and thirty-one.

If He Can't Do This Easily

Give him enough help to finish the task successfully, then ask three or four straightforward counting questions so he ends the oral session with success. Then move on to the written work.

If He Can Read the Numbers Correctly

You now need to find out if he really understands what the numbers mean. Don't just ask him directly. If he's one of the many people who find it difficult to think about numbers in abstract terms, he may not understand the question even if he does understand place value. Instead encourage him to talk about a specific number of objects rather than about the number itself. If he already understands place value, your conversation will sound something like this:

YOU: Let's think about that second number again. What shall we imagine we've got four hundred and fifty-two of? Carrots? Elephants? What would you like?

CHILD: Donkeys.

YOU: OK, so we've got four hundred and fifty-two donkeys. Look at the number two. (*Point at it.*) How many donkeys is that two telling us about?

CHILD (*probably looking at you as if you were mad*): Two.

YOU: That's easy, isn't it? Now how about the five? (*Point at it.*) How many donkeys is the five telling us about?

CHILD: Fifty.

YOU: Oh, you obviously know this really well already. But what about the four? How many donkeys is that telling us about?

CHILD: Four hundred.

YOU: Well done.

However, if he doesn't completely understand place value, your conversation may sound more like this:

YOU: How many donkeys is the five telling us about?

CHILD: Five.

YOU: Are you sure?

CHILD: I think so.

YOU: Think carefully. What did you say the whole number was?

CHILD: Four hundred and fifty-two.

YOU: So the five isn't telling us about five, is it? It's telling us about fifty. (*Take away the card with the two on it to show the fifty on the card below.*)

YOU: If you take away the next card, then you can tell me what the four is telling us about.

CHILD (*removes card with fifty on it*): Four hundred.

YOU: Well done.

Now ask your child to do some straightforward counting so he can end this part of the session with success before he tackles the written work.

Moving On
- If your child knew that the five meant fifty and the four meant four hundred, move on to step 4 for your next session.
- If your child couldn't read the numbers easily or could read them but didn't know what the five and the four meant, move on to step 2 for your next session.

Step 2

Aim
To teach your child the meaning of place value.

Before You Start the Session
Collect eighty-two pennies into a heap on the table (don't let your child see you counting them). Put the other coins a small distance away where they're clearly visible.

Tackling the Oral Work
The work for this step consists of two games which you can fit into your oral work so use the written part of the session for more practice with addition and subtraction.

REMEMBER
Don't rush. Time spent helping your child to really master this topic will pay dividends later.

Game 1
After you've begun the session with some counting work, show your child the pile of pennies. Talk about how heavy

they are. It would be hard work to take them all to a shop. Can he think of a way to make that amount of money lighter to carry?

If necessary, show him the other coins on the table and suggest they may help. You may need to remind him that one 10p coin is worth the same as ten pennies. Once he's realized that he could change some of the pennies into 10ps, help him to actually do it by giving him a 10p coin each time he gives you a pile of ten pennies.

When he's finished, talk about how many coins there are now. Your conversation might sound like this:

YOU: That's much better. I could carry them much more easily now and they're easier to count too. How many 10ps have we got?

CHILD: Eight.

YOU: And how many pennies are there in eight 10ps?

CHILD: Eighty. (*If necessary help him count in tens to work this out.*)

YOU: Good. (*Put the 80 card beside the 10p coins.*) Now how many penny coins have we got?

CHILD: Two.

YOU: That's right. (*Put the 2 card beside the pennies.*) So we've got eighty pennies and two pennies which is . . .? (*Put the 2 card on top of the 80 to show the answer.*)

CHILD: Eighty-two.

YOU: That's right. So the eight tells us how many 10ps we have and the two tells us how many pennies.

Repeat the whole exercise letting your child choose how large a pile of pennies to use. Let him write the numbers on the spare cards and overlap them to make the complete answer. Keep playing the game until he can easily change from pennies to 10ps and write the number without difficulty. Don't worry if this takes more than one session.

Extending Game 1

When your child can handle numbers of less than one hundred confidently, give him a pile of fourteen 10ps and two pennies. Once again, ask him to make the pile of coins lighter to carry. If he's not sure what to do, point out the £1 coins on the table and suggest they may help. Remind him that each £1 coin is worth one hundred and help him to count in tens to find how many 10p coins are worth the same as a £1 coin.

Once he's realized that he can change ten of the 10ps into £1, help him to do so and then show the total number of pennies by putting the cards on top of each other as you did before. Keep playing the game using numbers greater than one hundred until he can sort out the coins easily and confidently. Once again, this may take more than one session.

Game 2

When your child has mastered game 1, give him all the coins and declare that he's in charge of the bank.

Put the 8 card on top of the 30 to show the number thirty-eight. Tell him you want 38p from the bank but you're going to carry it a long way so you want it to be as light as possible (that is, using 10ps and pennies). You can add more fun to the game by suggesting an outlandish destination. If necessary, take the 8 card off the 30 so he can see how the number is made up and give him help or reassurance as he sorts out the coins.

Thank him when he gives you the right money and comment that the thirty-eight you asked for is made up from three 10ps (point to the 3) and eight pennies (point to the 8). Continue playing the game using other numbers less than one hundred until he can play it easily. Remember to only use numbers which can be made with the number of coins you have available.

Extending Game 2

Put the 40 card on top of the 200 and the 1 on top of the 40 to show the number two hundred and forty-one. Tell him that this time you need 241p (not £2.41), but it must still be as light as possible to carry. He may understand straight away and use two £1 coins. If he doesn't, suggest he lifts the top two cards to see what the 2 means and remind him that £1 worth a hundred pennies. Continue playing the game with numbers involving hundreds, tens and units until he can play it easily.

Moving On

Once your child can play both games confidently, move on to step 3.

Step 3

Aim

To develop the skills of writing, reading and understanding numbers greater than ten.

Before You Start the Session

Write this exercise in your child's book:

1)	$20 + 5 =$	11)	$200 + \quad + 3 = 243$
2)	$40 + 3 =$	12)	$300 + \quad + 7 =$
3)	$50 + \quad = 56$	13)	$700 + 60 + \quad = 764$
4)	$70 + \quad = 73$	14)	$400 + 30 + \quad = 437$
5)	$\quad + 8 = 48$	15)	$\quad + 60 + 6 = 266$
6)	$\quad + 3 = 23$	16)	$\quad + 50 + 1 = 951$
7)	$100 + 20 + 4 =$	17)	$\quad + \quad + 3 = 863$
8)	$300 + 70 + 3 =$	18)	$\quad + \quad + 6 = 756$
9)	$800 + 80 + 8 =$	19)	$700 + 70 + 7 =$
10)	$400 + 5 + 4 =$	20)	$300 + 30 + 3 =$

To write more exercises, make up similar questions by breaking numbers greater than ten into their component parts and leaving spaces for your child to fill. Only use numbers which don't contain any zeros when they are written in their unbroken form. For example, you can use 573 or 65 but not 760 or 609.

Tackling the Exercise
With this step, we return to written exercises for a while so you can go back to making up your own oral work.

When you show your child the written exercise, explain that you want him to fill in the spaces so that the sums are right. If he gets stuck, encourage him to think how he would use coins to make that number of pennies. Let him actually use the coins if he wishes. If you haven't got enough, you can tear up pieces of paper to stand in as extra pounds and 10ps.

When my child does this type of work at school, his teacher makes him draw pictures of numbers on an abacus. Is this important?

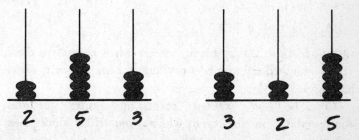

An abacus is just another method of showing place value. Personally I feel that drawing this type of picture is not as helpful as playing with coins but, if his teacher demands it, then it's got to be done. Help him to tackle the questions so he doesn't get into trouble at school and continue to use money at home to help him understand place value.

Moving On
Stay on this level until your child can answer the questions confidently and accurately. Then move on to step 4.

Step 4

Aim
To deal with the most common mistakes in reading and writing numbers greater than ten.

Before You Start the Session
Write this exercise in your child's book:

1)	$400 + 50 + 6 =$	11)
2)	$300 + \quad + 8 = 378$	12)
3)	$300 + 90 + \quad = 390$	13)
4)	$400 + 50 + \quad = 450$	14)
5)	$600 + \quad + 7 = 607$	15)
6)	$300 + \quad + 7 = 307$	16)
7)	$400 + 70 + 0 =$	17)
8)	$500 + 30 + 0 =$	18)
9)	$600 + 0 + 6 =$	19)
10)	$900 + 0 + 8 =$	20)

Questions 11 to 20 are blank because when he gets to these, you're going to say numbers out loud for him to write down in figures.

To write more exercises, make up similar questions, concentrating on the type which your child finds most difficult.

Tackling the Exercise
The first ten questions are the same as those in step 3 but they involve numbers containing a zero. We haven't included these before as they're a little more tricky but your child now understands place value well enough to be able to tackle them.

If he looks doubtful or worried, talk him through the questions to help him understand what to do. For example, in question 3, remind him that the three tells us about the three hundreds and the nine tells us about the nine tens. Then ask him how many ones the zero tells us about?

When he's finished those questions, read out the following numbers for him to write down in figures:

11) One hundred and thirty-two
12) Three hundred and ninety-six
13) Six hundred and seventy-three
14) Seven hundred
15) Seven hundred and fifty
16) Three hundred and four
17) Five hundred and one
18) Four hundred and sixty
19) Two hundred and ninety-eight
20) Eight hundred and thirty-three.

This work may seem trivially easy but it isn't. A surprisingly high number of children get in a muddle if asked to write two thousand, three hundred and forty-five and put 200030045. Even more make mistakes when asked to write three thousand and four. Spending time on this topic now will prevent your child making embarrassing mistakes at school and perhaps give him the satisfaction of finding he's better at something than some of his classmates.

If he finds the questions difficult, encourage him to think how many hundreds there are, how many tens and how many ones. Let him write down the individual parts added together as he did in the previous step to help him see what's happening. For instance, for question 11, he could write:

$$100 + 30 + 2 = 132$$

Moving On

Stay on this level until your child can answer both types of question confidently and accurately. Then move on to the next chapter.

14 / Adding and Subtracting Larger Numbers

Now your child understands place value, she's ready to start adding and subtracting numbers larger than ten. These sums look far more difficult than they really are. Your child already has all the skills she needs to tackle them so, once she understands what to do, she should be able to manage them fairly easily. This should give her confidence a huge boost.

Step 1

Aims
1) To introduce simple arithmetic with larger numbers.
2) To introduce the conventional method for setting down harder arithmetic questions.

Before You Start the Session
Write the exercise on the next page in your child's book. I've put the addition sign to the left of the bottom number but it's equally correct to put it to the right of the top number instead. Use whichever style your child prefers.

REMEMBER
Neatness is very important when questions are written with the numbers underneath each other like this. Set your child a good example by writing the questions neatly yourself.

---

1) 2 + 3 =

2) 20 + 30 =

3) 5 + 4 =

4) 50 + 40 =

5) 500 + 400 =

6) 3 + 6 =

7) 30 + 60 =

8) 300 + 600 =

9) 20 + 70 =

10) 10 + 30 =

11)   60
    + 20
    ──

12)   50
    + 30
    ──

13)   30
    + 40
    ──

14) 300
   + 200
    ──

15) 400
   + 300
    ──

To write more exercises, make up similar questions involving adding tens or hundreds. Write some one way and some the other.

Tackling the Exercise

If your child isn't sure how to tackle question 2, try changing it into words: 'If you have two tens already and you get another three tens, how many tens have you got altogether?' You can also illustrate what you're saying with 10p coins. Give similar help with each question until she's confident enough to manage without it.

─────────────────────────────────────

REMEMBER
Your child isn't being babyish if she uses coins, fingers or other equipment. Many adults, as well as children, find it much easier to understand a problem if they can actually see it rather than just imagine it.

─────────────────────────────────────

If your child looks worried when she reaches question 11, explain that this is just another way of writing maths. It's not magic or more difficult. In fact, the questions are exactly the same type as the ones she's just got right.

Despite all your reassurances, she may not believe you straight away. Let her use the coins if she wants to and be ready to help her, if necessary, by turning the questions into words. As she gains confidence, she'll gradually need less and less help.

Moving On
Stay on this level until your child can answer the questions confidently and accurately. Then move on to step 2.

Step 2

Aim
To introduce slightly harder addition questions.

Before You Start the Session
Write this exercise in your child's book:

1)	60 + 30 —	5)	34 + 43 —
2)	51 + 23 —	6)	64 + 35 —
3)	55 + 23 —	7)	53 + 14 —
4)	22 + 44 —	8)	46 + 23 —

$$9) \quad \begin{array}{r} 71 \\ + \underline{25} \\ \hline \end{array} \qquad 10) \quad \begin{array}{r} 32 \\ + \underline{23} \\ \hline \end{array}$$

To write more exercises, make up questions which involve adding together two numbers that are greater than ten but less than a hundred. Make sure that both the tens and the ones columns add up to less than ten.

Tackling the Exercise

If necessary, use coins to show your child what to do. For example, in question 2, give her five 10p coins and one penny. Then give her another two 10ps and three pennies and ask how many pennies she has altogether. Your conversation might sound like this:

CHILD: I've got seventy-four now.

YOU: Good. So now you've got the answer, we'd better write it down. Where shall we write the four?

CHILD (*doubtfully*): Hmmm?

YOU: Well, what's the four telling us about?

CHILD: Pennies.

YOU: That's right. You've got four penny coins. And where are the numbers in the question which tell you about ones or pennies?

CHILD: There. (*Pointing at the one and the three.*)

YOU: So where do you think you should put our number which tells us about pennies?

CHILD: Underneath. (*Writes the four in the correct place.*)

YOU: Good. And what do we get if we add one and three together?

CHILD: Four.

YOU: That's right. So that's another way we could have found the answer, isn't it?

CHILD: Yes.

YOU: Let's see if that would work for the tens as well.
Which two numbers in the question tell you about
tens?

CHILD: The five and the two.

YOU: And what do we get if we add the five and the two
together?

CHILD: Seven.

YOU: Great. So we've found we have seven tens by adding
the numbers and by counting the coins. Now where
do you think you should write that we've got seven
tens?

CHILD: There. (*Writes the seven in the answer under the five and
the two.*)

YOU: That's right.

Work with your child in this way for each question until she
understands what to do. Then gradually reduce your help as
she gains confidence.

REMEMBER
**These questions are so simple that your child will get the correct
answer whether she adds the ones first or the tens. However this
won't be true later on. Help her develop good habits by making
sure she always works out the answer from right to left (starting
with the ones). Ask her to read out the answer sometimes to make
sure she doesn't also get into the habit of reading the answer
backwards.**

Moving On
Stay on this level until your child can answer the questions
confidently with only occasional errors in the actual addition.
Then move on to step 3.

Step 3

Aim
To introduce subtraction of numbers larger than ten.

Before You Start the Session
Write this exercise in your child's book. You can put the subtraction sign to the right of the top number or to the left of the bottom one as I've done. Both methods are correct. Use whichever one your child prefers.

1)	70		6)	84
	− 30			− 52
	—			—
2)	56		7)	96
	− 22			− 53
	—			—
3)	78		8)	88
	− 26			− 55
	—			—
4)	94		9)	66
	− 62			− 43
	—			—
5)	49		10)	55
	− 17			− 34
	—			—

To write more exercises, make up similar subtraction questions where both numbers are less than a hundred. Make sure that the lower number in each column is smaller than the one above it.

Tackling the Exercise
When you first show your child the exercise, check that she's
noticed that these are subtraction questions. If she looks worried,
use coins to illustrate the questions. For example, for the second
question, you can give her five 10p coins and six pennies. Ask
her to give you 22p and tell you how many pennies she has
left. Then help her to write her answer in the correct place and
talk about how she could have worked out the answer by subtracting the numbers just as she added them in the previous exercise.

Moving On
Stay on this level until your child can answer the questions
easily and confidently with only occasional errors with the
subtraction. Then move on to step 4.

Step 4

Aim
To extend these methods to larger numbers.

Before You Start the Session
Write this exercise in your child's book:

$$
\begin{array}{lr}
1) & 45 \\
& +\ 23 \\
& \overline{}
\end{array}
\qquad
\begin{array}{lr}
4) & 86 \\
& -\ 35 \\
& \overline{}
\end{array}
$$

$$
\begin{array}{lr}
2) & 76 \\
& +\ 21 \\
& \overline{}
\end{array}
\qquad
\begin{array}{lr}
5) & 245 \\
& +\ 152 \\
& \overline{}
\end{array}
$$

$$
\begin{array}{lr}
3) & 45 \\
& -\ 25 \\
& \overline{}
\end{array}
\qquad
\begin{array}{lr}
6) & 567 \\
& -\ 262 \\
& \overline{}
\end{array}
$$

7)   685   9)   562
    − 472   + 321
    ─────   ─────

8)   999   10)   654
    − 932   − 221
    ─────   ─────

To write more exercises, make up addition and subtraction questions involving numbers less than a thousand. In the addition questions, make sure that neither the hundreds, tens or ones add up to more than nine. In the subtraction questions, make sure that the bottom figure in each column is smaller than or equal to the one above it.

Should I write the initials HTU above the columns as we did when I was at school?

Don't put the letters in when you first write the exercise. Your child may think they're a vital part of the question and believe they've magical powers which they don't possess. Also, if she doesn't need them, she may be insulted.

Wait and see how she copes with the questions. If she really is having trouble remembering which column is which, suggest she puts H above the hundreds column and T above the tens. (Putting U above the ones column only makes sense if you are talking about units.) Make sure she realizes the letters are only there to jog her memory. Then she'll feel free to leave them out as soon as she stops needing them.

Tackling the Exercise

Before you start, point out to your child that she'll have to read each question carefully as some are addition and some are subtraction. She may make the transition to larger numbers easily. If not, encourage her to think about money again with the hundreds column equivalent to pounds.

When she reaches question 8, she may write the answer as 062. If she does, congratulate her on finding the correct answer but ask her to look at it carefully. It says sixty-two but that's not how we usually write it. Explain that when the answer to the left-hand column is zero, we just leave a space.

Moving On

Stay on this level until your child always works from right to left and can answer the questions confidently with only occasional errors. Then move on to multiplication.

15 / Multiplication

Let me share a secret with you – a secret which may unlock many of the mysteries of mathematics – ALL MATHEMATICIANS ARE LAZY. Well, they're lazy about writing, anyway. They never write more than the basic minimum they can get away with. That's why mathematics is so difficult to understand when it's written down. It's not really a mystical language designed to hide the meaning of the universe from the uninitiated. It's just a form of shorthand designed to save physical effort, paper and ink.

Multiplication is one example of this shorthand in action. Multiplication means successive addition: adding the same number over and over again. 5 × 3 means the same as 3 + 3 + 3 + 3 + 3 or 5 +5 + 5 but it's much quicker to write. Unfortunately it's also scarier to read if you're not good at maths. It looks like a whole new process when it's really just a development of one already mastered.

The work in this chapter is designed to help your child understand what multiplication really means. Then he'll find it less frightening and be able to work out the answers when he can't remember his tables.

Step 1

Aim
To introduce multiplication.

Before You Start the Session
Write this exercise in your child's book. Arrange the work on the page so there's a space at least 1 cm wide to the left of it and enough room for another line of writing above it.

$$2 + 2 =$$
$$2 + 2 + 2 =$$
$$2 + 2 + 2 + 2 =$$
$$2 + 2 + 2 + 2 + 2 =$$
$$2 + 2 + 2 + 2 + 2 + 2 =$$
$$2 + 2 + 2 + 2 + 2 + 2 + 2 =$$
$$2 + 2 + 2 + 2 + 2 + 2 + 2 + 2 =$$
$$2 + 2 + 2 + 2 + 2 + 2 + 2 + 2 + 2 =$$
$$2 + 2 + 2 + 2 + 2 + 2 + 2 + 2 + 2 + 2 =$$

Tackling the Exercise
Start the session with some oral work as usual but make sure you include counting in twos so this number pattern is fresh in your child's mind. Then move on to the written exercise.

After the first few questions your child may start adding two to the previous answer instead of working out each answer from first principles, but don't worry if he doesn't do this. It doesn't mean he's stupid. He may have noticed the pattern but think he's not supposed to use it or he may just be one of the many people who find pattern spotting difficult.

When he's finished, mark the sums and praise his success. If he didn't notice the pattern while he was working, ask him if he can see it now. If he can't, ask him to say the answers out loud in the right order and help him to recognize that he's counting in twos.

From then on your conversation could run something like this:

YOU: Some of those sums are very long, aren't they? (*Child nods.*) That last one's particularly big. How many twos are there?

CHILD: Ten.

YOU: Shall I tell you a secret?

CHILD: Yes!

YOU: Well, mathematicians are very lazy. They don't like writing long sums like that. It's too much like hard work. Do you know what they do instead?

CHILD: No.

YOU: Instead of writing ten twos added together, they write this. (*Put 10 × 2 to the left of the last sum.*)

CHILD: But that's a times sign.

YOU: That's right. That's because we've added two ten *times*.

Continue talking in the same way as you write the correct question to the left of each line of twos. As your child gets the idea, he might like to write some of them in himself. When you have finished, write 1 × 2 = 2 on the spare line at the top to complete the pattern. The exercise should look like this:

$$1 \times 2 = 2$$
$$2 \times 2 = 2 + 2 = 4$$
$$3 \times 2 = 2 + 2 + 2 = 6$$
$$4 \times 2 = 2 + 2 + 2 + 2 = 8$$
$$5 \times 2 = 2 + 2 + 2 + 2 + 2 = 10$$
$$6 \times 2 = 2 + 2 + 2 + 2 + 2 + 2 = 12$$
$$7 \times 2 = 2 + 2 + 2 + 2 + 2 + 2 + 2 = 14$$
$$8 \times 2 = 2 + 2 + 2 + 2 + 2 + 2 + 2 + 2 = 16$$
$$9 \times 2 = 2 + 2 + 2 + 2 + 2 + 2 + 2 + 2 + 2 = 18$$
$$10 \times 2 = 2 + 2 + 2 + 2 + 2 + 2 + 2 + 2 + 2 + 2 = 20$$

Your child may recognize this as the two times table. If not, tell him this is what it is. Then either end the session there or, if you've plenty of time left, give him a few addition and subtraction questions like those from the last chapter.

Moving On
a) If your child already knew that multiplication means repeated addition, move on to step 2 for your next session.
b) If your child managed the addition easily but didn't already know what multiplication means, repeat this exercise in the next session adding fives instead of twos. If he still hasn't quite mastered the concept, go through the whole process again to produce the ten and three times tables. As soon as he understands what you are talking about, move on to step 2 for your next session.

Step 2

Aims
1) To produce a tables square to help your child with school work.
2) To reinforce the fact that multiplication is successive addition.

Before You Start the Session
Draw the grid on the next page on a piece of paper. Don't put it in your child's book as he may need to look at it during other sessions or take it to school.

Tackling the Exercise
Explain that you're going to make a tables square together. Your child will understand what to do if he's seen one before. If not, you'll have to explain.

Each box in the grid corresponds to a number on the top and a number on the side. Into each box you're going to put the answer you get when you multiply those two numbers together. Then any time you want to find the answer to a

X	0	1	2	3	4	5	6	7	8	9	10
0											
1											
2											
3											
4											
5											
6											
7											
8											
9											
10											

multiplication question, you've just got to look for it in the appropriate box.

Fill in the table a row at a time working from left to right so your child can work out the answers by adding. Start with the row that corresponds to the one as that's the easiest and fill in the zero row last. When you've finished it should look like this:

×	0	1	2	3	4	5	6	7	8	9	10
0	0	0	0	0	0	0	0	0	0	0	0
1	0	1	2	3	4	5	6	7	8	9	10
2	0	2	4	6	8	10	12	14	16	18	20
3	0	3	6	9	12	15	18	21	24	27	30
4	0	4	8	12	16	20	24	28	32	36	40
5	0	5	10	15	20	25	30	35	40	45	50
6	0	6	12	18	24	30	36	42	48	54	60
7	0	7	14	21	28	35	42	49	56	63	70
8	0	8	16	24	32	40	48	56	64	72	80
9	0	9	18	27	36	45	54	63	72	81	90
10	0	10	20	30	40	50	60	70	80	90	100

While you're working, help your child to notice that two numbers multiplied together always give the same answer regardless of which one we write first (for example, $5 \times 4 = 4 \times 5$ and $7 \times 9 = 9 \times 7$).

My child insists that 2 × 0 is 2. How can I persuade him that it isn't?

Multiplying by zero or nought often causes problems and is yet another case when it helps to use coins to show what's going on. It also sometimes helps if you use the word 'nothing' instead of nought. Try putting two piles of three pennies on the table and talking to your child like this:

YOU: Suppose I gave you these two piles of three. How many pennies would you have?

CHILD: Six.

YOU: That's right. Two threes are six. Now how many would you have if I gave you one pile?

CHILD: Three.

YOU: Right. One three is three. So how about if I was feeling mean and kept them all. How many would you have if I gave you no piles at all?

CHILD: None.

YOU: Great. So no threes are nothing, aren't they?

You can also explain it by approaching the problem from the other direction. Mime making several piles of nothing in front of you. Don't worry if you're not the world's best actor: ham it up and play for laughs. Your conversation might sound like this:

YOU: I'm feeling really generous today. I'm going to give you one of my piles of nothing. (*Mime handing it over.*) Now, how much have you got?

CHILD: Nothing.

YOU: Oh, dear. That's not much. I'd better give you some more. Have another of my piles of nothing. There – you've got two lots of nothing now. That must be better. How much have you got?

CHILD: Nothing.

YOU: Oh, dear. You've still not got anything. So two lots of nothing are nothing. Well I'd better give you another pile of nothing. That should help. (*Mime handing it over – continue as long as you both want.*)

Moving On
When your child has successfully completed the tables square, move on to the next chapter.

Does my child need to learn his tables?

Yes. Unless he can multiply small numbers together from memory, he'll find it difficult to cope with harder work. The tables square is only a first aid measure to help him cope with school work involving the tables he hasn't yet learnt. Let him take it to school and use it for homework while you help him fill in the gaps in his knowledge.

DEVELOPING THE ORAL WORK 3   Tackling Tables

There are several different ways to help your child learn his multiplication tables. Use as many of them as you can because practising tables easily becomes boring if you don't vary your approach.

Concentrate on one table at a time and let your child master it before you introduce another. Start with the two times table then move on to the ten, five, three and four times tables in that order. When your child has learnt those, introduce the six, seven, eight and nine times tables in any order which you choose.

Method 1 Counting in Patterns
Counting forwards and backwards in twos, threes, etcetera is a valuable preliminary to learning tables. It helps build a mental picture of the numbers in relation to each other and speeds up your child's ability to work out any answers he's forgotten. Never introduce a table without first practising the appropriate number pattern.

Method 2 Reciting Tables

By this I mean the traditional chant of 'One two is two, two twos are four, three twos are six . . .' which has been heard in classrooms for generations. It certainly has a place in learning tables but don't make the mistake of seeing it as an end in itself. Your child doesn't need to be able to chant his tables out loud. (If you don't believe me, think when you last had to do it.)

What he needs to be able to do is answer individual multiplication questions. Reciting tables helps some children gain this skill. For others, the actual process of recitation causes so much trouble that they never really get to grips with the maths. If your child finds reciting tables difficult, try saying the first part for him like this:

YOU: One two is . . .
CHILD: Two.
YOU: Two twos are . . .
CHILD: Four.
(*etcetera*)

BY THE WAY
There are several ways of saying tables. 'Two twos are four' and 'two times two are four' are the most common while saying 'two lots of two are four' emphasizes the connection between multiplication and addition. All are equally correct so use whichever method your child prefers.

Method 3 Simple Questions

Once your child can count in the appropriate number pattern, you can ask him simple questions like 'What are three twos?' or 'What is five times two?'

If he doesn't know the answer from memory, let him work it out by counting in the appropriate pattern or saying the appropriate table. This is better than looking up the answer in his table square as it's more likely to help him remember the answer.

Simple written questions such as $3 \times 2 = \quad$ and $5 \times 3 = \quad$ also give good practice with tables so include some in your revision work.

Method 4 Games and Puzzles

There are music tapes and videos which help children memorize their tables, plus computer games and electronic games which give good practice in simple multiplication. You could also make your own pairs games based on tables questions (see chapter 9). Beware of anything which seems too young: your child may be offended if you give him something he considers babyish.

Memory Tricks

People often use interesting facts and mental tricks to help them remember their tables. Here are some you can mention to your child. You may know some others yourself.

- All the answers to the ten times table end in zero.
- All the answers to the five times table end in five or zero.
- The answer is the same regardless of the order you multiply the numbers so $8 \times 3 = 3 \times 8$ etcetera.
- The figures in all the answers to the nine times table add up to 9 (for example, $2 + 7 = 9$ and $3 + 6 = 9$)

This last fact leads to a fascinating way of showing the nine times table on your fingers. Hold up both hands, palms towards you. Imagine the fingers are numbered from one to ten, starting on the left.

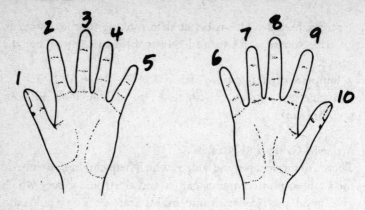

To find the answer to any question from the nine times table, fold down the finger corresponding to the number you wish to multiply by nine. The number of fingers to the left of it tells you how many tens there are in the answer. The number of fingers to the right tells you how many units. So if you want to work out 4 × 9, fold down finger number four.

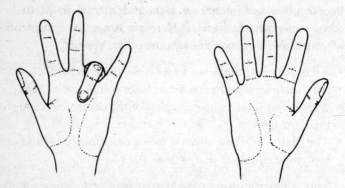

There are three fingers to the left of it and six to the right, so the answer is thirty-six. In the same way, if you want to work out 8 × 9, fold down finger number eight.

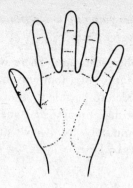 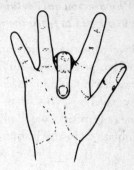

There are seven fingers to the left of it and two to the right, so the answer is seventy-two. It's amazing, isn't it, but it really does work for the whole nine times table. If you don't believe me, try it and see.

REMEMBER
Different people think in different ways so don't assume that your child will find the same tricks helpful that you do. Let him decide for himself which ones he wants to use.

My child is dyslexic and I've been told he'll never learn his tables.

The world is full of people who have been told they would never do something and who have proved the pessimists wrong. Your child may find it hard to learn his tables, but it's worth persevering. Even if he only learns some of them, it'll be better than nothing. Don't worry if he finds reciting his tables particularly difficult because he loses his place. Counting in patterns will help his memory and speed up his ability to work out the answers he's forgotten.

Why are you only talking about tables going up to ten times when I had to learn them all up to twelve times?

Twelve was a more important number years ago. There were twelve pennies in a shilling, twelve inches in a foot and many items were sold in dozens, so we needed to be able to multiply by twelve. Now that we use decimal money and metric measurements, we don't have to multiply by twelve often enough to justify learning the answers by heart.

16 / Addition Again

Congratulations on getting this far. Your child now has a good understanding of place value and multiplication and can answer straightforward addition and subtraction questions easily so she should be feeling much more confident with numbers. All your hard work is having effect so give yourself a pat on the back and move confidently on to the work that lies ahead.

Your child can already cope happily with simple addition sums: ones where neither the hundreds, tens or ones add up to more than nine. It's now safe for you to remove that restriction and move on to sums which involve carrying.

BE PREPARED

If your child has failed to understand this topic in the past, she may panic when she realizes what you are asking her to do. Be prepared to boost her confidence and assure her that she now knows enough to master this step quite easily.

Step 1

Aim
To revise the background skills your child needs to cope with this topic.

Before You Start the Session
Write the exercise on the next page in your child's book:

1)	8 + 2 =	11)	5 + 5 =
2)	6 + 8 =	12)	8 + 5 =
3)	7 + 5 =	13)	8 + 8 =
4)	9 + 4 =	14)	9 + 3 =
5)	3 + 8 =	15)	9 + 9 =
6)	7 + 7 =	16)	7 + 4 =
7)	6 + 7 =	17)	9 + 8 =
8)	5 + 6 =	18)	8 + 7 =
9)	2 + 9 =	19)	5 + 9 =
10)	6 + 6 =	20)	1 + 9 =

To write more exercises, make up addition questions where the numbers to add together are less than ten but the answer is ten or more.

Tackling the Oral Work

After you've started the session with a few counting exercises, give your child two 10p coins and seven pennies. Then give her another 10p and eight pennies and ask her how much she has altogether. Your conversation might sound like this:

> YOU: Count up and see how much you have now.

CHILD: 45p.

> YOU: Good. But it's heavy to carry, isn't it? Can you think what you could do to make it lighter?

CHILD (*looks blank*): No.

> YOU: Do you remember what we did before? You got very good at changing piles of pennies into 10ps.

CHILD (*smiles as she remembers*): Oh, yes. I can take ten of these (*takes away ten pennies*) and change them for one of those (*puts back one 10p*).

> YOU: So, what coins have you got now?

CHILD: Four tens and five pennies.

> YOU: Good. And it's much easier now to see that you've got 45p.

Play this game a few more times using different amounts of money. Then move on to the written work.

Tackling the Exercise
This exercise is designed to practise simple addition sums whose answers are greater than ten. Don't worry if your child has to use her fingers to work out answers which she previously knew by heart. She's only forgotten facts which she hasn't been using lately, just as you and I do. The extra practice she'll get in this chapter will soon have her adding even better than before.

Moving On
Stay on this level until your child can change the coins easily in the oral work and can answer the written questions confidently and accurately (with or without using her fingers). Then move on to step 2.

Step 2

Aim
To introduce addition sums where the ones column adds up to more than ten.

Before You Start the Session
Write this exercise in your child's book:

$$
\begin{array}{llll}
1) & \begin{array}{r} 45 \\ +\ \underline{32} \\ \overline{} \end{array} & \qquad 3) & \begin{array}{r} 37 \\ +\ \underline{51} \\ \overline{} \end{array} \\[3em]
2) & \begin{array}{r} 64 \\ +\ \underline{25} \\ \overline{} \end{array} & \qquad 4) & \begin{array}{r} 45 \\ +\ \underline{27} \\ \overline{} \end{array}
\end{array}
$$

5)	54	8)	76
	+ 39		+ 16
	—		—
6)	49	9)	38
	+ 34		+ 42
	—		—
7)	57	10)	52
	+ 36		+ 33
	—		—

To write more exercises, make up questions which involve adding two numbers which are larger than ten but smaller than one hundred. In most of the questions, make the numbers in the ones column add up to ten or more. In all the questions, make the numbers in the tens column add up to less than nine.

Tackling the Exercise
The first three questions should not cause your child much trouble as they are the same as she was doing in chapter 14. Make sure she works them from right to left as this is vital for the rest of the exercise.

When she starts question 4, she'll find that the numbers in the ones column add up to twelve. She may competently use the carrying method to write the two in the ones column and put the one below the lower answer line in the tens column like this:

$$\begin{array}{r} 45 \\ +27 \\ \hline 72 \\ {\scriptstyle 1} \end{array}$$

Alternatively she may put the carrying number just above the top answer line like this:

$$
\begin{array}{r}
45 \\
+\,27 \\
\hline
72
\end{array}
$$

Either method is perfectly all right provided it works for her. Let her go on and finish the question and then continue with the rest of the exercise.

USING THE RIGHT WORDS
The common way to describe this process is to say 'Put down the two and carry one.' But you are not carrying one, you are carrying ten. It's better to say 'Put down the two in the ones column and put the ten in the tens column.'

If your child doesn't know how to deal with the twelve in question 4, she may either look blank or come up with ideas which don't work, like squeezing both figures into the ones column. If she's met carrying before but not really understood it, she may suggest putting the one in the ones column and the two under the lower answer line in the tens column.

At this point it's important not to take the easy way out and just tell her what to do. That will solve the immediate problem but teaching her a trick will only work until she forgets it again. To get this method firmly in her head, she needs to understand what she's doing and that means going back to first principles so she can work out what to do herself.

Get out the coins again and make two piles: one of four 10ps and five pennies and the other of two 10ps and seven pennies.

Your conversation might sound like this:

YOU: Those two piles make a picture of that sum, don't
         they? (*If you wish you can arrange the coins in two rows
         so they look like the question.*)

CHILD: Yes.

YOU: So how many penny coins have we got?

CHILD: Twelve.

YOU: That's right. Now, can you remember what we were
         doing the other day? How can we make those twelve
         pennies lighter to carry?

CHILD: Swop ten of them for a 10p?

YOU: And then you'd have . . .?

CHILD: One 10p and two pennies.

YOU: Good. That's what twelve means – one ten and two
         ones. Perhaps remembering that will help you write
         down that twelve you don't know what to do with.

CHILD: Will it?

YOU: Well, the two ones can go in the ones column. (*Write
         in the two.*)

$$\begin{array}{r} 45 \\ +\ 27 \\ \hline 2 \end{array}$$

And where does the ten belong?

CHILD: Ummm.

YOU: Well, where are the other numbers that tell us about
         tens? (*Child points at the four and the two.*) That's right.
         So the right place for our ten is in the same column,
         isn't it?

CHILD: Yes, but if we put it next to the two it'll be in the
         way of the answer.

YOU: I'm really pleased you noticed that. Not everyone does straight away. So we need somewhere to put it where we won't forget it when we add up the tens but where it won't be in the way either. Let's put it underneath the bottom line like this.

$$\begin{array}{r} 45 \\ + 27 \\ \hline 2 \\ \hline 1 \end{array}$$

CHILD (*surprised*): I remember Mrs Brown doing that sometimes but I didn't understand what she was talking about.

YOU: That's because you weren't ready to learn about it then but you are now because you are getting good at maths. Can you add up the tens?

CHILD: Six.

YOU (*whispers*): Oops. Don't forget the one at the bottom.

CHILD: Is it seven?

YOU: Yes. Well done. Now we just need to put that in the right place, like this.

$$\begin{array}{r} 45 \\ + 27 \\ \hline 72 \\ \hline 1 \end{array}$$

So what's the answer?

CHILD: Seventy-two.

YOU: Great. Now try the next one.

Once you've successfully completed question 4, work through the rest of the exercise together giving your child as much help as she needs. As she gains confidence, allow her to gradually take over until she's working alone (this is likely to take more than one session). Whenever she gets stuck, encourage her to think of how she would tackle the question if the numbers were money. Let her use real coins if she wishes.

My child keeps putting numbers the wrong way round so, if she's trying to deal with fifteen, she puts the one in the ones column and the five in the tens column.

This is a very common mistake. First of all, make sure that she really understands what she's doing. If necessary, go back to using coins so she can see that the one in fifteen is one ten so it needs to go in the tens column.

If she continues to make the same mistake when you're sure she understands the method, try encouraging her to write the carrying number in the tens column before she writes the other number in the ones column. That way she'll still be writing the tens number first, just as she would if she were writing the number normally.

My child writes the carrying number in the right place but then forgets to add it on.

That's something we all do from time to time so try not to lose your temper. Just remind her gently when she forgets and suggest she crosses out the carrying number once she's added it on.

Moving On
Stay on this level until your child can answer the questions easily with only occasional help to avoid mistakes. Then move on to step 3.

DON'T RUSH
The concept your child is learning in step 2 is vital. Once she understands it, she'll be able to apply it without further trouble to many apparently harder questions. Take your time and don't move on until you're sure your child knows what she's doing. If you're in doubt, it's better to stay on this level too long rather than move on too quickly.

Step 3

Aim
To introduce addition questions where the numbers in the tens column add up to ten or more.

Before You Start the Session
Write this exercise in your child's book:

1)	135 + 243	6)	277 + 232
2)	342 + 429	7)	326 + 281
3)	287 + 361	8)	346 + 463
4)	155 + 163	9)	343 + 182
5)	370 + 243	10)	543 + 345

To write more exercises, make up similar addition questions using numbers between 100 and 999. The numbers in the hundreds column should add up to eight or less but those in either the tens column or the ones column (but not both) can add up to ten or more.

Tackling the Exercise

When your child reaches question 3, she'll find that the numbers in the tens column add up to more than ten. If she's not sure what to do, encourage her to use the same technique as she did when the ones column added up to ten or more. If necessary, use real coins to help her see exactly what's happening. Your conversation might sound like this:

YOU: So how many tens have you got altogether?

CHILD: Fourteen, but that's too big to write in the answer.

YOU: So what are you going to do?

CHILD: Don't know.

YOU: Well, what would you do if it was the ones column that added up to fourteen?

CHILD: I'd write the four in the ones place and put the one underneath the line in the tens place.

YOU: That's right. Because the fourteen is made up of four ones and one ten and that ten needs to be with the other tens. But this time we haven't got fourteen ones to deal with. We've got fourteen tens. That's four tens and ten tens, isn't it?

CHILD: Yes.

YOU: And what are ten tens?

CHILD: One hundred.

YOU: So that one in the fourteen is really one hundred, isn't it?

CHILD: Yes.

YOU: And where are the other numbers which tell us about hundreds?

CHILD: There. (*Points to the two and the three*.)

YOU: So that one should be with them in the hundreds column, shouldn't it?

CHILD: Yes. Do I write it underneath like I did before?

YOU: Yes, otherwise it will get in the way. Don't forget to write the four in the tens column too. Now, how many hundreds are there altogether?

CHILD: Six.

YOU: Well done. You remembered to add on the extra one underneath. I'm really pleased at how quickly you're getting the hang of this.

Continue to help in this way with each question until your child is confident enough to start working alone.

USING THE RIGHT WORDS
In question 3, you talked about writing the four tens in the tens column and the one hundred in the hundreds column. Once your child is working alone, she'll probably prefer to say 'Put down the four and write the ten in the next column.' Although this is not such a true account of what's happening, it's quite acceptable. To help her remember what's really happening, you can occasionally remind her that the ten is actually ten tens and that's why it needs to go in the hundreds column.

Moving On
Stay on this level until your child can answer the questions confidently with only occasional mistakes. Then move on to step 4.

Step 4

Aim

To introduce slightly more difficult questions.

Before You Start the Session

Write this exercise in your child's book:

1)	245 + 546 ———	6)	166 + 777 ———
2)	363 + 462 ———	7)	275 + 596 ———
3)	678 + 255 ———	8)	354 + 544 ———
4)	277 + 394 ———	9)	76 + 76 ———
5)	85 + 66 ———	10)	379 + 416 ———

To write more exercises, make up addition questions where the two numbers to be added together are both between 10 and 999 and the numbers in the hundreds column add up to less than ten. In the majority of the questions, make both the tens column and the ones column add up to ten or more.

Tackling the Exercise

Although these questions are slightly more difficult than the previous ones, they don't involve any new skills. The only complication is that sometimes both the tens and the ones column add up to ten or more. This may surprise your child so much that she initially thinks she's made a mistake. Once she realizes that she hasn't, the questions shouldn't cause her much trouble but be prepared to help her if she gets in a muddle.

When she reaches question 5, she'll find that she has one hundred which she's carried from the tens column but there are no other hundreds to add to it. Once again, be ready to reassure her that she hasn't made a mistake.

Moving On

Stay on this level until she can answer the questions confidently with only occasional mistakes. Then move on to step 5.

Step 5

Aim:

To introduce questions where the hundreds column adds up to ten or more.

Before You Start the Session

Write this exercise in your child's book:

$$
\begin{array}{ll}
1) & \begin{array}{r} 256 \\ +\ \underline{349} \\ \hline \end{array} \qquad
3) & \begin{array}{r} 452 \\ +\ \underline{743} \\ \hline \end{array} \\[2em]
2) & \begin{array}{r} 463 \\ +\ \underline{374} \\ \hline \end{array} \qquad
4) & \begin{array}{r} 653 \\ +\ \underline{542} \\ \hline \end{array}
\end{array}
$$

5)	647	8)	1649
	+ 539		+ 2724
	—		—

6)	583	9)	567
	+ 748		+ 356
	—		—

7)	678	10)	354
	+ 456		+ 445
	—		—

To write more exercises, make up similar questions where the two numbers to be added together are both between one hundred and 999 and the hundreds column adds up to ten or more. If you wish, you can include some questions where the numbers are larger than a thousand but the thousands column adds up to less than nine.

Tackling the Exercise

Now your child has mastered the previous steps, the process of carrying ten hundreds (or a thousand) will present few problems. If she's not sure what to do or gets in a muddle, talk her through the question as you did in step 3.

Moving On

When your child can answer these questions competently and confidently, move on to step 6.

Step 6

Aim
To introduce questions where your child will need to carry more than one ten or one hundred.

Before You Start the Session
Write this exercise in your child's book:

1)	11 + 9 + 14 —		5)	118 + 39 + 14 —
2)	26 + 18 + 24 + 33 —		6)	191 + 92 + 30 —
3)	45 + 16 + 29 —		7)	23 + 47 + 17 —
4)	36 + 26 + 18 —		8)	16 + 19 + 34 —

To write more exercises, make up questions adding three or four numbers together. In the majority of the questions, make either the tens column or the ones column (or both) add up to twenty or more.

Tackling the Exercise

These sums are nowhere near as difficult as they look. Answering them successfully will give your child's confidence an enormous boost. If she looks worried when she first sees them, reassure her that she's very good with numbers now and will be able to answer them without much trouble.

She may look confused when she finds, in question 2, that the ones column adds up to twenty-one. If so, reassure her that she hasn't made a mistake. Then remind her that the two in twenty-one is telling her about two tens so she has two tens to move into the tens column. She'll probably be able to understand that without using coins but let her use them if she wishes.

Moving On

Stay on this level until your child can answer the questions confidently and accurately. Then move on to chapter 17.

DEVELOPING THE ORAL WORK 4

By the time your child reaches chapter 18, she needs to have a reasonable grasp of her two times, five times and ten times tables. It doesn't matter if she doesn't know them all by heart but she should be able to quickly and confidently work out any answers she can't remember, so include some practice with these tables in your oral sessions while you work through chapter 17 (unless the step you are on suggests something else).

Number Stories

To add variety to your tables work, you can use number stories which involve multiplication. Here are two to get you started:

- 'Julie is cooking a surprise for all the family. The recipe says she needs two apples for each person. If there'll be four

people eating the meal, how many apples does she need?'
- 'Mrs Baker bought both her children a giant inflatable elephant. If each one cost £5, how much did she spend?'

Remember to keep the multiplication easy by using the tables your child knows well.

17 / And Back to Subtraction

Now your child has completely mastered addition, it's time to move on to subtraction questions like

$$
\begin{array}{r}
8\,3 \\
-\,5\,9 \\
\hline
\end{array}
$$

The straightforward method from chapter 14 runs into trouble here because the top number in the ones column is smaller than the bottom one.

There are two methods of tackling this type of question. The first is called subtraction with borrowing and is quite possibly the method you were taught at school. To deal with the fact that you can't take nine away from three, you borrow one from the tens column to make the three into thirteen. Then you give back the ten you borrowed by adding one to the bottom number in the tens column. The working looks like this:

$$
\begin{array}{r}
8\,{}^{1}3 \\
-\,{}^{6}\!5\,9 \\
\hline
2\,4 \\
\end{array}
$$

Don't worry if you've never seen this method before. You won't be teaching it to your child so it doesn't matter if you don't understand it.

If you already use this method successfully yourself, that's fine. Feel free to go on using it but don't try to teach it to your child. It's almost certainly not the method he will be taught in school so it'll just confuse him.

Most schools now teach the second method which is called subtraction by decomposition. (Don't be frightened of the name: it's just a word and your child doesn't need to know it.) In this method you still change the three into thirteen but this time you do it by breaking up (or decomposing) the eighty-three. Instead of writing it as eight tens and three ones, you change it to seven tens and thirteen ones. The working looks like this:

$$\begin{array}{r} 7\,\overset{1}{\cancel{8}}\,3 \\ -\ 5\ 9 \\ \hline 2\ 4 \end{array}$$

If you compare the way the two sums are written down, you will understand why some parents complain that their children are being taught to subtract upside down.

DON'T PANIC
If you haven't met this second method before, you're probably feeling fairly confused by now. Don't worry. You'll soon get the hang of it if you work through the rest of this chapter by yourself. Make sure you understand the method clearly before you try to help your child.

Why have schools decided that the second method is better?

The problem with subtraction with borrowing is that it's difficult to explain what's really happening. That's why it's taught as a trick. It's a very effective trick, of course. You'll get the right answer every time if you remember what to do but that's a big if. If you can't remember the trick, you're lost. There's no easy way to work it out for yourself.

In contrast, subtraction by decomposition is a logical application of place value. If you give your child some coins and point him in the right direction, he'll work the method out for himself. Once he really understands what he's doing, he's unlikely to forget it. Even if he does, he'll be able to work it out again from scratch.

Perhaps my child's school is very old fashioned. Despite all you've said, he's still been taught to use the first method you've described. Should I teach him the other way?

Not if he's confident and successful using the method he's already learnt. However, if he's having trouble with it or makes many mistakes, explain that you're going to show him another method which is easier. Then follow the instructions in this chapter to teach him to use decomposition instead.

Step 1

Aim
To practise the background skills your child needs for the work in this chapter.

Before You Start the Session
Write this exercise in your child's book:

1)	$11 - 2 =$	6)	$13 - 4 =$
2)	$14 - 6 =$	7)	$18 - 9 =$
3)	$11 - 4 =$	8)	$11 - 5 =$
4)	$12 - 7 =$	9)	$12 - 4 =$
5)	$16 - 9 =$	10)	$13 - 8 =$

11) $15 - 7 =$ 16) $15 - 6 =$
12) $12 - 5 =$ 17) $13 - 6 =$
13) $11 - 3 =$ 18) $15 - 9 =$
14) $14 - 5 =$ 19) $14 - 8 =$
15) $17 - 9 =$ 20) $12 - 3 =$

To write more exercises, make up similar subtraction questions where the first number is between ten and nineteen, the second number is less than ten and the answer is nine or less.

Tackling the Exercise

This exercise is designed to give your child practice with subtracting numbers less than ten from numbers between ten and twelve. He'll frequently have to do this when he's solving subtraction questions by decomposition, so it's important that he can do it easily.

The questions shouldn't cause him much trouble as he met similar ones in chapter 12. However, he's probably not done many since then so don't worry if he has to work out answers which he could previously remember. The extra practice will soon refresh his memory.

Moving On

Stay at this level until your child can answer the questions confidently and accurately (with or without using his fingers). Then move on to step 2.

Step 2

Aim

To introduce the idea of decomposition by using coins.

Before You Start the Session

Write some multiplication questions in your child's book.

Tackling the Oral Work

Put a pile of pennies and 10p coins in the middle of the table. Give your child five 10p pieces and four pennies. Then ask him to give you 37p. If you weave a funny story around your request, you'll make the game more enjoyable. Your conversation might sound like this.

YOU: Aren't you lucky, having so much money. And look at me. I've got nothing at all and I'm so thirsty. If you give me 37p, I can have a drink.

CHILD: Here you are. (*Gives you 40p.*)

YOU: (*give it back*): But I don't want 40p. I want 37p.

CHILD: You can give me some change.

YOU: No, I can't. Look at me. I haven't any money for change. I need exactly 37p.

CHILD: But I haven't got that.

YOU: Well, you could get the bank to help. (*Point at the pile of coins.*)

CHILD: Here you are then. (*Takes 37p from the bank and gives it to you.*)

YOU (*give it back*): Oops. You can't just take money out of the bank without putting any in. Quick, you'd better put it back before they realize they've been robbed.

CHILD: (*Laughs and puts coins back in pile.*)

YOU: I'm still ever so thirsty. I could really do with that 37p. Why can't you give it to me?

CHILD: I haven't got enough pennies.

YOU: Well, how about changing one of your other coins into pennies at the bank.

CHILD: That's easy! (*Changes a 10p into pennies and gives you 37p.*)

Play this game several more times using different stories and different numbers but always ask for more pennies than your child has available. Then use the rest of the session to tackle the written multiplication questions.

Moving On
a) If your child knew what to do without any help from you, move on to step 3 at your next session.
b) If your child needed help before he realized what to do, stay on this level for at least one more session. When your child can always give you the amount you need without difficulty, move on to step 3.

Step 3

Aim
To apply decomposition to written questions.

Before You Start the Session
Write this exercise in your child's book:

$$
\begin{array}{ll}
\text{1)} & 48 \\
& -\,23 \\
\hline
\end{array}
\qquad
\begin{array}{ll}
\text{4)} & 473 \\
& -\,147 \\
\hline
\end{array}
$$

$$
\begin{array}{ll}
\text{2)} & 37 \\
& -\,15 \\
\hline
\end{array}
\qquad
\begin{array}{ll}
\text{5)} & 252 \\
& -\,134 \\
\hline
\end{array}
$$

$$
\begin{array}{ll}
\text{3)} & 42 \\
& -\,26 \\
\hline
\end{array}
\qquad
\begin{array}{ll}
\text{6)} & 65 \\
& -\,28 \\
\hline
\end{array}
$$

7)	78	9)	86
	− 59		− 58
	—		—

8)	552	10)	68
	− 247		− 46
	——		—

To write extra exercises, if necessary, make up similar subtraction questions where both numbers are between ten and 999. In most of the questions, make the bottom number in the ones column larger than the top one. In all the questions, make the bottom number in the tens and hundreds columns smaller than the top one.

BE CAREFUL
Don't make all the questions involve decomposition or your child may start to believe he should always use it.

Tackling the Exercise
The first two questions are straightforward so should present no real problems. Question 3 is more difficult so work with your child to avoid the risk of failure. If he knows what to do, you can gradually reduce the amount of help you're giving him and let him continue with the rest of the exercise by himself.

If he doesn't know how to tackle this question successfully, reassure him that most people find this type of question difficult at first but you're confident that he'll be able to manage them. As you work the first question with him, your conversation might sound like this:

YOU: Let's look at the ones column first. What's two take away six?

CHILD: Four.

YOU: Are you sure?

CHILD: Yes.

YOU (*give child two pennies*): Let's look at it with pennies. You've got two. Now can you give me six?

CHILD: No.

YOU: Well, can I take six?

CHILD: No! I haven't got six. I've only got two.

YOU: So let's look at the question again. We can't take six away from two here either, can we?

CHILD: No.

YOU: That's a problem then. But in the question you haven't just got two. You've got forty-two. (*Give child four 10p coins.*) That's just like the game we were playing the other day. Now, can you give me six?

CHILD: That's easy. (*Changes one 10p into pennies and gives six to you.*)

YOU: Good. Now let's look at that question and see if we can write down what you did. You took one of the tens and made it into ones. So we can cross out the four and make it one less, which is . . .?

CHILD: Three.

YOU: Good. So we'll write that down so we don't forget.

$$\begin{array}{r} \overset{3}{\cancel{4}}2 \\ -\ 26 \\ \hline \end{array}$$

Then you put the ten ones with the two you already had which gave us . . .?

CHILD: Twelve.

YOU: So we can make the two into a twelve by putting the ten beside it.

$$^{3}\cancel{4}{}^{1}2$$
$$-\underline{2\,6}$$

Now what do we have left, if we take six away from twelve.

CHILD: Six.

YOU: And is that how many pennies you had left?

CHILD: Yes.

YOU: Good. So we know that's right then. Put the six in the ones space in the answer.

$$^{3}\cancel{4}{}^{1}2$$
$$-\underline{2\,6}$$
$$6$$

That's great. We're really getting somewhere now. All you've got to do is find how many tens there are. You had three to start with and you've taken away two, so how many are left?

CHILD: One.

YOU: That's right. There's one ten left so write that down in the tens place.

$$^{3}\cancel{4}{}^{1}2$$
$$-\underline{2\,6}$$
$$1\,6$$

So what's the answer?

CHILD: Sixteen.

YOU: Well done. Let's try another one.

REMEMBER

Always talk about taking a ten from the tens column. Don't say you are borrowing it: you've no intention of giving it back. But don't worry if you've talked about borrowing in the past. You won't have done any harm.

Continue in this way for each question. Be patient. This isn't an easy technique to learn but it's a very important one. You may need to work with your child for quite a long time before he feels confident enough to work on his own. Let him use the coins as much as he likes. He'll probably find it much easier to understand what he's doing if he can see it happening with real objects.

Even when your child starts working on his own, he may still explain what he's doing by talking about 10p and pennies rather than tens and ones. Don't worry. That's all right. All that matters is that he understands the method he's using.

Moving On

Stay on this level until your child can answer the questions confidently with only occasional errors. Then move on to step 4.

AND NOW FOR THE GOOD NEWS

Once your child has completed this step, you've finished the really difficult part of this chapter. He has mastered the basic technique he needs for this type of question and just needs to practise using it in a variety of situations.

Step 4

Aim

To introduce the use of decomposition to calculate the tens column.

Before You Start the Session

Write this exercise in your child's book:

1)	245 − 123	6)	736 − 483
2)	356 − 137	7)	636 − 363
3)	246 − 162	8)	157 − 75
4)	217 − 184	9)	973 − 682
5)	136 − 84	10)	567 − 345

To write more exercises, make up questions which ask your child to subtract a number between ten and 999 from a larger one between one hundred and 999. Include a few questions which don't require decomposition. In the others, make the top number in the tens column smaller than the bottom one. In all the questions make the top number in the hundreds and the ones columns larger than the bottom one.

Tackling the Exercise

The first two questions are the type your child can already manage so they shouldn't cause much trouble. When he reaches question 3, he'll find that this time it's the tens column in which the bottom number is larger than the top one. He may realize straight away that he can use decomposition. If not, he'll need your help to see that he can change one of the hundreds into ten tens.

Encourage him to think about the problem in terms of money again. Give him two £1 coins, four 10ps and six pennies and ask him to give you two pennies. He'll manage that without any trouble.

Now ask him to give you six 10p coins. When he can't, suggest that perhaps he could change one of his pounds into 10p coins just as he changed a 10p into pennies before. Your conversation would be very similar to the sample one in step 3.

After he's worked out the sum with coins, help him to write down his working like this:

$$\begin{array}{r} {}^{1}\cancel{2}{}^{1}46 \\ -\ 1\ 6\ 2 \\ \hline 8\ 4 \end{array}$$

Continue working with him (using coins when necessary) until he is confident enough to work on his own.

Moving On

Stay on this level until he can answer the questions accurately and confidently without using coins. Then move on to step 5.

Step 5

Aim
To introduce slightly more difficult questions.

Before You Start the Session
Write this exercise in your child's book:

1)	567 − 145	6)	635 − 276
	——		——
2)	754 − 426	7)	753 − 469
	——		——
3)	826 − 464	8)	444 − 366
	——		——
4)	765 − 478	9)	531 − 444
	——		——
5)	731 − 375	10)	726 − 555
	——		——

To write more exercises, make up subtraction questions where both numbers are between one hundred and 999. Include one or two which require no decomposition. In the others, make the top number smaller than the bottom number in either the tens column, the ones column or both. In all the questions, make the top number in the tens column greater than zero and the top number in the hundreds column larger than the bottom one.

Tackling the Exercise

The first three questions are similar to the ones your child has answered successfully before, so they shouldn't cause much trouble. When he reaches question 4, he should manage to subtract the ones column easily by taking a ten from the tens column to make the five into fifteen.

$$\overset{5}{\cancel{7}}\overset{'}{\cancel{6}}5 \\ -478$$

When he starts to work out the tens column, he'll be surprised to find that the top number is smaller than the bottom one again. If he looks worried, reassure him that he hasn't made a mistake and encourage him to keep working out the answer in the same way as he has previously.

$$\overset{6}{\cancel{7}}\overset{15}{\cancel{6}}\overset{'}{5} \\ -478 \\ \overline{287}$$

As always, if he becomes confused, encourage him to think how he would work out the sum if he was using money and let him use coins to help him if he wishes.

REMEMBER
It is particularly important to encourage your child to do this work neatly. Untidiness can cause mistakes.

Moving On
Stay on this level until your child can answer the questions confidently with only occasional mistakes. Then move on to step 6.

Step 6

Aim
To introduce the final complication: zeros in the top number.

Before You Start the Session
Write this exercise in your child's book:

1)	586 − 372	6)	8307 − 3188
2)	670 − 348	7)	5606 − 3844
3)	204 − 158	8)	6004 − 3746
4)	300 − 176	9)	9003 − 2638
5)	803 − 684	10)	8586 − 7474

To write more exercises, make up subtraction questions using numbers between one hundred and 9999. Make most of the questions involve decomposition and have at least one zero in the top number.

Tackling the Exercise

The first two questions shouldn't cause your child much trouble. However in question 3, when he tries to take a ten from the tens column, he'll find there aren't any there. If he's not sure what to do, give him two £1 coins and four pennies and ask him to give you 158p. If necessary, help him to realize that he needs to change one of the pounds into 10p coins and then change one of the 10ps into pennies.

Then suggest that he tries the same approach with the written question by taking one of the hundreds and making it into ten tens.

$$
\begin{array}{r}
{}^1\!\cancel{2}\,{}^1\!0\;4 \\
-\,1\;5\;8 \\
\hline

\end{array}
$$

He can then take one of the tens and make it into ten ones so he can work out the answer.

$$
\begin{array}{r}
{}^1\!\cancel{2}\,{}^{\;9}\!\cancel{0}\,{}^1\!4 \\
-\,1\;5\;8 \\
\hline
4\;6
\end{array}
$$

Keep helping him as much as necessary until he gains enough confidence to work alone.

Question 6 introduces thousands. Your child may be daunted by the size of the numbers but the actual subtraction shouldn't present any problems.

In question 7 he'll need to take one of the thousands and turn it into ten hundreds before he can work out the hundreds column. If he doesn't realize this straight away, encourage him to think how he would tackle the question if it was money and the thousands were £10 notes.

The final complication arises in question 8 but your child doesn't need any new skills to solve it: just perseverance, patience and neat writing. Be prepared to work with him if he seems worried.

The problem is that he can't take a ten because there aren't any and he can't take a hundred either. What he needs to do first is take one of the thousands and turn it into hundreds.

$$
\begin{array}{r}
\overset{5}{\cancel{6}}\overset{\prime}{0}04 \\
-\ 3746 \\
\hline
\end{array}
$$

Then he can take one of the hundreds and turn it into tens.

$$
\begin{array}{r}
\overset{5}{\cancel{6}}\overset{9}{\cancel{0}}'04 \\
3746 \\
\hline
\end{array}
$$

Finally he can take one of the tens, turn it into ones and then work out the answer.

$$
\begin{array}{r}
\overset{5}{\cancel{6}}\overset{9}{\cancel{0}}\overset{9}{\cancel{0}}'4 \\
-\ 3746 \\
\hline
2258
\end{array}
$$

Moving On
Stay on this level until your child can answer the questions confidently with only occasional mistakes but don't worry if he still works quite slowly. Then move on to chapter 18.

REVISION IS IMPORTANT

You and your child have now worked through a large part of this basic arithmetic section but he needs regular practice to prevent him forgetting the skills he's gained. You can provide this by giving him a few revision questions in each exercise and/or by giving him occasional exercises which only involve previous work. If you find he's forgotten something, go back to that level for a few sessions until he's remembered it again.

Try writing some of the questions across the page like this:

$$345 + 176 = \text{ instead of like this} \quad \begin{array}{r} 345 \\ + \underline{176} \\ \hline \end{array}$$

Encourage your child to rewrite each question with the numbers underneath each other before he works it out.

Developing Your Revision Work

As your child masters new skills with numbers, you'll need to increase the amount of revision work you do. In particular, before your child starts a new stage of work in Section 3 spend some time going over the background knowledge he requires so it's fresh in his mind.

REMEMBER

When the work I suggest is designed to fit into the oral part of the session, use a revision exercise as the written work.

---

18 / More Multiplication

Because multiplication is successive addition, the technique of carrying used in multiplying large numbers by small ones is essentially the same as that used in addition. However, your child may not realize this if the actual multiplication is so difficult that she becomes bogged down in the mechanics of the question. To avoid this happening, the sample questions in this chapter only ask her to multiply by two, five or ten (the tables she has been practising in your oral sessions). Once she understands how to tackle this work, you can introduce questions involving the other tables she knows.

Step 1

Aim
To introduce questions involving multiplying large numbers by small ones.

Before You Start the Session
Write this exercise in your child's book:

```
1)    31              2)    31
    + 31                  ×  5
    + 31                    ──
    + 31
    + 31    ──→
      ──
```

3)   22
  + 22
  + 22
  + 22
  + 22
   —

$\longrightarrow$

4)   22
  × 5
   —

5)   13
  + 13
  + 13
  + 13
  + 13
   —

$\longrightarrow$

6)   13
  × 5
   —

7)   54
  + 54
  + 54
  + 54
  + 54
   —

$\longrightarrow$

8)   54
  × 5
   —

This exercise is a special introductory one. You won't need to write any more like it.

Tackling the Exercise
When you show your child the exercise, point out that you have numbered the questions differently from usual, so question 2 is to the right of question 1 instead of underneath it.

The first question is straightforward so your child should manage it easily. Question 2 is the first multiplication sum you have given her which involves a number larger than ten.

If she manages to answer question 2 without help, she's either been taught this before or is automatically applying her previous knowledge to this new task. Ask her if she can see any

connection between this question and the one before. If necessary, help her to see that they are both the same question but
written in different ways: thirty-one multiplied by five means
the same as five thirty-ones added together.

If she doesn't know what to do or looks worried, ask her if she
can see any connection between this question and the one
before. If necessary, look back to the original work you did on
multiplication to remind her that multiplying is the same as
adding the same number over and over again.

When she's realized that both questions are the same, suggest
that she could work out question 2 in the same way as she did
question 1. Instead of adding the five ones together, she can
multiply the one by five. Then, instead of adding together the
five threes in the tens column, she can multiply the three tens
by five.

$$\begin{array}{r} 31 \\ \times\ \underline{5} \\ \underline{155} \end{array}$$

Repeat this approach for the rest of the exercise.

Moving On
Your child will probably have understood the connection
between the two types of question by the end of this exercise
but don't worry if she's still a little doubtful. There will be
plenty of opportunities to repeat the explanation in further
exercises so move on to step 2 in your next session.

Step 2

Aim
To provide further practice at multiplication.

Before You Start the Session
Write the following exercise in your child's book:

1)	34	6)	143
	× 2		× 5
	—		—

2)	53	7)	75
	× 2		× 5
	—		—

3)	36	8)	286
	× 2		× 2
	—		—

4)	74	9)	127
	× 2		× 5
	—		—

5)	34	10)	23
	× 5		× 2
	—		—

To write more exercises, make up similar questions which involve multiplying a number greater than ten by two, five or any other number for which your child knows the table.

Tackling the Exercise
These questions are the same type as in the previous step so, provided your child understands the method to use, she should be able to answer them without much trouble.

If your child's still a little unsure of the method, be prepared to work with her for as long as she needs you to. At first, as you tackle each question, write out the equivalent addition question on a separate piece of paper so she can see the connection between the two methods. As she gains competence and confidence, you can gradually reduce the amount of help you give until she's able to manage on her own.

Moving On
Stay on this level until your child can answer the questions confidently with only occasional mistakes. Then move on to step 3.

Extending Multiplication
As your child learns her other tables, remember to include questions involving them in your revision work.

DEVELOPING THE ORAL WORK 5

Now you're sure that your child can confidently add, subtract and multiply, you can introduce some puzzle questions into your oral work. These will help to reinforce the idea that subtraction is the opposite of addition and division is the opposite of multiplication. Here are some sample ideas to get you started.

- I think of a number, I add two and the answer's seven. What is the number?
- I think of a number, I take away three and the answer is five. What is the answer?
- I think of a number, I multiply it by two and the answer is eight. What is the number?

Only use quite small numbers until your child understands what to do. She'll probably enjoy asking you similar questions too and that will help her maths just as much.

Later on when she understands division, you can introduce questions like:

- I think of a number, I divide it by two and the answer is five. What is the number?

Number Magic

Try this on your child:

> Choose a number between one and five but don't tell me what it is.
>
> Now add three to it but don't tell me the answer.
>
> Now take away one. (Still don't tell me.)
>
> Now take away the number you first thought of.
>
> And I know your answer is two.

She's sure to be amazed and you can impress her again and again if you like, using different instructions each time. Keep the numbers small enough for her to cope with easily. The effect is lost if she makes a mistake.

The secret is to always ask her to take away the number she first thought of. Then it doesn't matter that you don't know what it is. You can just find the answer by working out the addition and subtraction you told her to do as if the original number was zero. For instance, in my example, you added three and you took away one, so the answer is two.

When your child is really confident with multiplication and division, you can introduce those skills into the trick too. Make sure that if you ask her to multiply by a number, you later ask her to divide by it again *before* you ask her to take away the number she first thought of, otherwise the trick won't work. You also need to be careful to choose the numbers you ask her to add and subtract in such a way that the division you ask her to do will give a whole number without a remainder as an answer.

Here is an example to get you started:

> Think of a number between one and five.
>
> Add three.
>
> Multiply it by two.
>
> Add two.
>
> Divide by two.
>
> Take away the number you first thought of.

The answer is four.

I leave it up to you to decide whether to keep the secret of the trick to yourself or to share it with your child.

19 / Introducing Division

Division is the poor relation in maths. It's taught after addition, subtraction and multiplication (as it is here) and usually has far less time devoted to it. That's why so many people feel less confident about dividing than they do about the rest of number work.

DON'T PANIC
If you are not happy about division yourself, you've probably been dreading this chapter. Don't worry. We're going to move through this subject very slowly. You'll be fine if you read each step carefully before you tackle it.

Talking about Division

The most common way of introducing division is through the idea of sharing. So 12 ÷ 3 becomes 'If John has twelve sweets to share between himself and his two sisters, how many will they have each?'

However, sharing is not the only way to describe division so it's not a good idea to concentrate on it exclusively. Later on in his school career, your child will have to divide by fractions and it's just not possible to share sweets between half a person.

The other way to think about division is as multiple subtraction: how many times you can take one number away from a larger one. So 12 ÷ 3 becomes 'How many piles of three bricks can you take from a pile of twelve bricks?' Of course, people don't often need to do that so you may prefer to wonder how many things costing 3p each you could buy with 12p.

Writing it Down

One complication of division is that it can be written in several different ways. For instance, twelve divided by six can either be written as

$$12 \div 6$$

or

$$6\overline{)12}$$

or

$$\frac{12}{6}$$

The first method matches how a question would be worked out on a calculator. It's commonly used in computer games and textbooks. The second method is particularly useful when you're working out the answer to a division question without a calculator. The third method is used a great deal in more advanced work, especially algebra. However, your child needs to understand fractions before he can use it, so we're not going to introduce it in this chapter. You'll find more about this method in chapter 22.

It's important that your child realizes that the first two methods are alternative ways of writing the same questions and can use them both confidently. That's why most of the exercises in this chapter use a mixture of both styles. However, once he starts working with larger numbers in the next chapter, it will be better for him to use the second method all the time.

Step 1

Aim
To introduce division as the opposite of multiplication.

Before You Start the Session
Write this exercise in your child's book:

1)	2 × ☐ = 4		9)	5 × ☐ = 35
2)	3 × ☐ = 6		10)	☐ × 2 = 8
3)	☐ × 5 = 20		11)	4 × ☐ = 40
4)	10 × ☐ = 60		12)	☐ × 10 = 80
5)	7 × ☐ = 14		13)	8 × ☐ = 16
6)	☐ × 2 = 18		14)	5 × ☐ = 25
7)	5 × ☐ = 45		15)	☐ × 10 = 90
8)	5 × ☐ = 15		16)	5 × ☐ = 5

To write more exercises, make up similar questions involving the multiplication tables which your child already knows.

Tackling the Exercise
If necessary, explain that you want your child to fill in the gaps to make the answers correct. Don't use the word divide while you are talking about this work unless he uses it first. Instead, if you need to turn any of the questions into words, use phrases like 'How many twos make four?' or 'How many piles of three can you make with six?'

If your child hasn't met division very much before, he may find it difficult to apply his tables knowledge in this way. If necessary, encourage him to work out the answers with the help of his fingers or some coins. This will give him a better understanding of division than he would gain from looking up the answers on his tables square.

REMEMBER
There's nothing babyish about using coins or fingers to learn a
new skill. Forcing your child to work entirely in his head before he
is ready will just make him confused and damage his confidence.

Moving On
Stay on this level until your child can answer the questions
confidently and accurately (with or without using his fingers).
Then move on to step 2 in your next session.

Step 2

Aim
To introduce the two common ways of writing division
questions.

Before You Start the Session
Write this exercise in your child's book:

1)	$6 \div 2 =$	9)	$15 \div 3 =$
2)	$20 \div 5 =$	10)	$12 \div 1 =$
3)	$2 \overline{) 14}$	11)	$5 \overline{) 40}$
4)	$5 \overline{) 35}$	12)	$2 \overline{) 18}$
5)	$40 \div 10 =$	13)	$15 \div 5 =$
6)	$8 \div 4 =$	14)	$16 \div 2 =$
7)	$10 \overline{) 80}$	15)	$5 \overline{) 30}$
8)	$5 \overline{) 45}$	16)	$10 \overline{) 30}$

To write more exercises, make up division questions involving
the tables your child already knows. Only use questions where
the smaller number divides exactly into the larger one and the

answer is less than ten. Write some of the questions in one way and some in the other.

Tackling the Exercise
Before your child looks at the exercise, talk to him about the two different ways of writing division questions. Your conversation might sound like this:

YOU: Let's think about this question.
(*Write 2 ×   = 12 on the paper.*)
What's it asking you?

CHILD: How many twos make twelve?

YOU: And what's the answer?

CHILD: Six.

YOU: Good. Now, if we wanted to, we could write that question like this.
(*Write 12 ÷ 2 = 6.*)

CHILD: That's a divide. I don't like divides. They're too hard.

YOU: Perhaps they used to be but they're not now. It's only another way of writing the question you just answered. It's still asking you 'How many twos are there in twelve?' and the answer's still . . .?

CHILD: Six.

YOU: Great. So you can do questions that look like that. Now what if I write it like this instead.
(*Write 2⟌ 12.*)

CHILD: That's how we write them at school and I can't do those either.

YOU: But you can now. Remember it's just another way of writing the questions you've been doing. It still means how many twos in twelve and the answer's still . . .?

CHILD: Six.

(*Write in the answer like this: 2⟌ 12.*)

BE CAREFUL

The six is telling you about six ones so it's important that you put it in the ones position above the two like this:

$$
\begin{array}{r}
6 \\
2\overline{)12}
\end{array}
$$

Not in the tens position like this:

$$
\begin{array}{r}
6 \\
2\overline{)12}
\end{array}
$$

Make sure your child always writes his answers in the correct place too.

Once you've introduced both methods of writing division questions, you can let your child start the exercise. The actual division shouldn't cause him much trouble but he may have problems coping with the different ways of setting down the work. If so, help him turn each question into words so he can see it's only the same as the ones he's previously answered successfully.

Moving On

Stay on this level until your child can easily answer the questions whichever way they are written down. Then move on to step 3.

Step 3

Aim

To introduce the idea of remainders.

Before You Start the Session

Write this exercise in your child's book:

1) $5\overline{)25}$

2) $2\overline{)5}$

3) $32 \div 10 =$

4) $15 \div 2 =$

5) $2\overline{)19}$

6) $27 \div 5 =$

7) $5\overline{)33}$

8) $10\overline{)74}$

9) $46 \div 5 =$

10) $47 \div 10 =$

11) $2\overline{)13}$

12) $18 \div 2 =$

To write more exercises, make up similar questions involving the tables your child already knows. In most of them, make the smaller number not divide exactly into the larger one. Write some of the questions in one style and some in the other.

Tackling the Exercise

When he reaches the second question, he'll find he can't divide five exactly by two. If he's not sure what to do, talk about the fact that, in real life, numbers often don't divide exactly and how we react to this depends on the situation we're in.

If we're dividing five cakes between two people, we'd probably give them two each and then cut the last one into two pieces. However, if we're sharing out books, it would be more sensible to take turns reading the one left over than to ruin it by tearing it in half.

The same is true in maths: there's more than one way to deal with a question which doesn't divide exactly. Sometimes we use fractions or decimals but, at the moment, we're just going to write down how many are left over. We call this the remainder. So for question 2, we write

$$2 \text{ remainder } 1$$
$$2\overline{)5}$$

Most people usually shorten remainder to rem or just r. Let your child choose which he wants to use.

Moving On
Stay on this level until your child can do the division and find the remainder confidently and accurately. Then move on to chapter 20.

DEVELOPING THE ORAL WORK 6

Now your child understands division, you can start to introduce it into your oral work. Keep the numbers small at first and only use the tables he knows well. You can start with questions like:

- What must I multiply two by to make six?
- How many twos make six?
- What do I get if I divide six by two?

Once he can cope with straightforward questions like these, you can begin to use some number stories. Here are two to get you started.

- The teacher told five children to move all the chairs out of the classroom. If there were thirty chairs altogether, how many did each of the children have to move.
- Gemma bought ten strawberry sweets as presents for her friends. If she spent 50p, how much did each sweet cost?

20 / Division Again

Your child now has all the skills she needs to divide larger numbers. Even if she's met questions like 635 ÷ 5 before, the chances are very high that she doesn't really understand how to tackle them.

That's because this topic is often taught in a rush. Many teachers wrongly assume that their pupils now understand place value so well that there's no need to go back to first principles at this stage. Instead they teach them a trick without really explaining why it works and those pupils who forget the trick are totally lost.

To avoid falling into the same trap, you're going to introduce this topic in oral work first by playing with coins just as you did when you started adding and subtracting larger numbers. While you're doing this, your child can continue to practise simple division in her written work.

Step 1

Aim
To introduce the idea of dividing large numbers.

Tackling the Oral Work
Start the oral work with a few counting exercises. Then give your child two £1 coins, six 10ps and eight pennies and ask her to divide the money between you. Encourage her to share out the pounds first, then the 10ps and leave the pennies until last.

After she's done this successfully, give her three £1 coins, five 10ps and six pennies and ask her to do the same thing again. This time she won't find it so straightforward as the number of pounds and ten pences don't divide exactly by two. If she's not sure what to do, encourage her to see that she could deal with the problem by changing one type of coin into another. Your conversation might sound like this:

CHILD: We can have one pound each (*gives them out*) but there's one left over. Who should I give that to?

YOU: It doesn't sound very fair for either of us to have it. We wouldn't both have the same then. What would you do with an odd one if you were sharing out cakes?

CHILD (*grins*): Eat it!

YOU: Come on. You're supposed to be fair. What would you really do with an odd cake?

CHILD: Cut it in two and give us half each.

YOU: Can you cut the pound in half?

YOU: No. It's too hard.

YOU: And I don't expect you could spend half a pound coin. Have another think.

CHILD: Hmmm. (*Looks blank.*)

YOU: Here's a clue. How many 10ps make a pound?

CHILD: Ten.

YOU: Is there some way that knowing that could help you?

CHILD: Umm. Could I change the pound into 10ps?

YOU: That sounds like a good idea.
(*Take the pound. Give her ten 10p coins.*)
How many tens have you got now?

CHILD: Fifteen.
(*Shares them out giving you seven each.*)
Oh! I've got the same problem. There's a 10p left over.

YOU: Could you do the same sort of thing again?

CHILD: Yes.

(*Changes the 10p into ten pennies and gives you eight each.*)
There! I've done it.

YOU: Well done.

Play the game a few more times before moving on to the written work. Choose any amounts which she can divide into two without any pennies left over.

Moving On
Stay on this level until your child can divide any amount into two without any difficulty. Then move on to step 2.

Step 2

Aim
To introduce written questions which involve dividing larger numbers.

Before You Start the Session
Write this exercise in your child's book:

1) $2 \overline{)\, 246}$ 6) $5 \overline{)\, 555}$

2) $2 \overline{)\, 428}$ 7) $2 \overline{)\, 660}$

3) $2 \overline{)\, 68}$ 8) $2 \overline{)\, 248}$

4) $2 \overline{)\, 84}$ 9) $5 \overline{)\, 550}$

5) $2 \overline{)\, 286}$ 10) $2 \overline{)\, 800}$

To write more exercises, make up questions dividing numbers greater than ten by either two or five. In each question, make sure each figure of the number can be divided exactly without any remainders.

Tackling the Exercise

These questions introduce division questions involving larger numbers without the complications of carrying. Because they only involve dividing by two and five, they allow your child to concentrate on understanding the method without becoming bogged down in difficult arithmetic.

If your child isn't sure how to tackle question 1, give her two £1 coins, four 10ps and six pennies and point out that the question is a written-down version of the tasks she's been handling happily in your oral work. Encourage her to tackle it in the same way and help her to write down what she's doing. Your conversation might sound like this:

YOU: So let's start by looking at the pounds first as you usually do. If you share those out between both of us, how many will we each have?

CHILD: One.

YOU: That's right. We've shared out the two hundred pennies so we have a hundred each and we can write that down like this.

$$2 \overline{\smash{)}\,246} \quad \overset{1}{}$$

We put the one above the two to show we mean one hundred. Now what happens when you divide the tens between us?

CHILD: We get two each.

YOU: Right. Now which number in the question shows us how many tens we had to start with?

CHILD: The four.

YOU: So where do you think we should put the number that tells us how many tens there are in the answer?

CHILD: Above the four?

YOU: Very good. So what number do we need to write in there?

CHILD: The two.

  YOU: Put it in then.

$$\overset{\textstyle 1\,2}{2\overline{)2\,4\,6}}$$

Now all you've got to do is divide the six ones between us. How many do we have each?

CHILD: Three.

  YOU: And where are you going to write the three?

CHILD: Just above the six.

  YOU: That's right. You put the three ones in the ones place.

$$\overset{\textstyle 1\,2\,3}{2\overline{)2\,4\,6}}$$

So the answer's 123. Does that match what you got when you worked it out with the coins?

CHILD: Yes.

Encourage your child to tackle the remaining questions in the same way, letting her use the coins to help her for as long as she wishes.

Moving On

Stay on this level until your child can answer the questions confidently without using coins. Then move on to step 3.

Step 3

Aim

To introduce division questions involving carrying.

Before You Start the Session

Write the exercise on the next page in your child's book:

1)	2)268	6)	2) 368
2)	2) 76	7)	2) 746
3)	2) 54	8)	5) 655
4)	5) 75	9)	5) 535
5)	5) 80	10)	2) 446

To write more exercises, make up questions which involve dividing numbers greater than ten by either two or five. Choose numbers where either the tens figure or the hundreds figure (but not both) cannot be divided exactly. To avoid remainders, make the numbers to be divided by two end with zero, two, four, six or eight and the numbers to be divided by five end with zero or five.

Tackling the Exercise

When your child reaches question 2, she'll realize that the seven in the tens position doesn't divide exactly by two. If she's not sure what to do, give her seven 10p coins and six pennies and ask her to divide them between you. Your conversation might sound like this:

YOU: Try dividing those coins between us. How many 10ps will we have each?

CHILD: Three and there'll be one left over.

YOU: And what can we do with that?

CHILD: Change it into pennies.

YOU: And how many pennies will we have then?

CHILD: Sixteen, so we'll have eight each.

YOU: Good. So now we know you're good enough at maths to do the question. All you need to do is work out how to write down what you are doing. Let's start with the tens. When we divided the seven tens by two, we each had three of them. Where do you think you should write those three tens?

CHILD: Above the seven, like this?

$$2\overline{)7\ 6}^{\ 3}$$

YOU: That's right.

CHILD: But what do I do with the one left over?

YOU: With the coins, you took the one ten and turned it into ten ones. You could write down the ten like this, so you can see that you have sixteen ones.

$$2\overline{)7\ '6}^{\ 3}$$

CHILD: And do I put the eight above the six.

YOU: That's right. The eight ones go in the ones place and then we can see the answer is thirty-eight.

$$2\overline{)7\ '6}^{\ 3\ 8}$$

Repeat this process with each question until your child is confident enough to manage without help. When it's the hundreds figure which doesn't divide exactly, help her to see that she can turn the leftover hundreds into tens in the same way as she turns the tens into ones.

CHOOSING THE RIGHT WORDS
I haven't used the word carrying in my explanation but there's nothing wrong with doing so, provided you use it correctly. Remember that you never carry one (or two or three . . .) You always carry one ten or one hundred (or two tens or two hundreds . . .).

Moving On
Stay on this level until your child can answer the questions accurately and confidently without using coins. Then move on to step 3.

Step 4

Aim
To practise dividing large numbers by small ones.

Before You Start the Session
Write this exercise in your child's book:

1)	5) 605	6)	5) 825
2)	5) 565	7)	2) 752
3)	5) 735	8)	5) 482
4)	2) 356	9)	2) 132
5)	2) 983	10)	2) 824

To write more exercises, make up similar questions which ask your child to divide by any number less than ten for which she knows the table. Let some, but not all, of the answers involve a remainder. The easiest way to think up questions which divide exactly is to work out a multiplication question first with a calculator. For example:

> Think of a number: 79
> Multiply by eight: 632
> Write the question:

$$8\overline{)\,632}$$

Tackling the Exercise

The first two questions are straightforward so she shouldn't find them too much trouble. Question 3 is slightly more complicated as neither the hundreds nor the tens figures can be divided exactly by five. If your child looks worried or isn't sure what to do, talk her through the question. Your conversation might sound like this:

YOU: How many fives are there in seven?

CHILD: One and there's two left over.

YOU: Fine, so write the one in the hundreds position in the answer and turn the two hundreds left over into twenty tens, so we've got twenty-three tens altogether.

$$5\overline{)\,7^{2}3\,5}\quad^{1}$$

Now, how many fives are there in twenty-three?

CHILD: Four and three left over.

YOU: That's right, so put the four in the tens position in the answer. Then turn the three tens into thirty ones, so we've got thirty-five ones altogether.

$$5\overline{)\,7^{2}3^{3}5}\quad^{1\,4}$$

YOU: Now, how many fives are there in thirty-five?

CHILD: Seven.

YOU: Good, so write the seven in the ones position in the answer and we can see that 735 divided by five is . . .

$$5 \overline{)7^2 3^3 5} \quad \begin{array}{c} 1\ 4\ 7 \end{array}$$

CHILD: 147.

Continue to help your child for as long as necessary. Be prepared to reassure her that she hasn't made a mistake when she finds that question 5 doesn't divide exactly and, if necessary, remind her how to write down the remainder. Also, for questions 8 and 9, you may need to remind her that we don't usually write zeros to the left of a number, so she should just leave a space in the hundreds position.

Moving On

Stay on this level until your child can answer these questions confidently and accurately. Then move on to any topic you wish to tackle from Section 3.

CONGRATULATIONS

You and your child have now worked successfully through the whole of basic arithmetic. She now has the basic skills she needs for the rest of mathematics (although she may still need to work a little at her tables).

You both have every right to feel pleased with yourselves. Your child's proved that she's good at maths after all and you've proved that you're capable of helping her. Why not make the most of your success? Ditch the next session and celebrate instead.

SECTION 3

21 / Time

When I was at school, I learnt to tell the time by looking at where the big hand and the little hand were pointing. Time has ticked on since then and it's no longer just recorded by the moving hands of traditional (or analogue) clocks. Digital clocks are taking over. My house contains nine of them compared with only two of their traditional competitors.

The popularity of digital clocks has changed the way we talk and write about time. Although people still speak of quarter past three and twenty to ten, they often say three fifteen or ten forty instead. It's particularly important that your child understands this second method as it's the way in which times are usually written in maths.

Some children (especially dyslexic ones) find it very difficult to learn to use a traditional clock. If your child is one of them, encourage him to use a digital clock instead. I also suggest you use a digital clock if he hasn't yet started to tell the time. Once he understands the principles of time, you can introduce the mysteries of the big hand and the little hand. To do this, you'll need a clock face with movable hands. You can either make one from card, buy a cheap one from a toy shop or, best of all, use an old clock with the glass removed.

Telling the Time

Step 1

Aims
1) To teach your child to tell the time on a digital clock.
2) To teach your child how we measure time.

Essential Background Knowledge
Before your child starts this work he should:
a) be able to recognize numbers
b) be able to count to sixty.

Equipment
You'll need a digital clock or watch.

Tackling the Oral Work
Because some of this work needs to be done at particular times of day, it's better to fit it into everyday conversation rather than to include it in your maths sessions.

To tell the time with the digital clock, your child only needs to read the numbers exactly as they appear. Explain that the numbers to the left of the dot or colon tell us how many hours and the numbers to the right tell us how many minutes. We read the two numbers separately so 11:45 is eleven forty-five, not one thousand, one hundred and forty-five.

Mention that the whole hours are special. When the clock shows 11:00, we say it's eleven o'clock or eleven, not eleven zero zero. Watch the clock together towards the end of an hour (but not just before 1 pm). Play guessing when the minute number will change to give your child a feel for how long a minute lasts.

At the end of the hour, make sure your child notices that the minutes change from fifty-nine to zero zero (not sixty) and that the hour number changes at the same time. Explain that when the clock has counted sixty minutes, that's a whole hour, so the clock moves the hour number on one and starts to count the minutes from zero again.

Once he understands this, you can encourage him to watch while the clock changes from 12:59 to 1:00. (Check in advance that it isn't set to the twenty-four-hour system.) Use this to help you explain that we usually divide the day into two twelve-hour periods.

Step 2

Aim
To show your child how to read whole hours from a traditional clock.

Essential Background Knowledge
Before starting this work your child should:
a) be able to recognize numbers
b) know that time is measured in hours and minutes.

Tackling the Oral Work
You can fit this and the rest of the work on telling the time into the oral part of your maths sessions. Look at your clock face together and talk about the way the big hand counts the minutes while the little hand counts the hours. Each time the big hand goes right round, that's one more hour, so the little hand moves to the next number. If you've a real clock, your child can experiment with turning the big hand and watching the little hand move.

Explain that when the big hand points at the twelve, it hasn't counted any minutes in the next hour. That's the same as when the minutes' number on the digital count says zero zero, so the time is something o'clock. The little hand tells us which o'clock it is.

Demonstrate this by moving the hands to show one o'clock.

Then play a game with your child where you show times for him to read or you tell him times to show on the clock.

Moving On
Stay on this level until your child can play the game without any mistakes. Then move on to step 2 or another topic.

Step 2

Aim
To teach your child to read half past, quarter past and quarter to from a traditional clock.

Essential Background Knowledge
Before starting this work your child should:
a) be able to read whole hours from a traditional clock
b) have a basic understanding of halves and quarters.

Tackling the Oral Work
You're going to introduce this work in four stages but don't feel you must fit all of them into one session. There is no need to rush, so only move on to the next stage when your child has mastered the previous one.

Stage 1
Start with both hands on your clock face pointing to the twelve. Move the big hand round until it points at six. Talk about it having gone halfway round the clock face. The distance it has travelled to the six is the same as it'll have to travel to get back to the twelve.

Tell your child that this time is called half past twelve because it's halfway between twelve o'clock and one o'clock. Use the clock face to practise half past different hours by showing times for your child to read and saying times for him to show on the clock.

Stage 2
Start again with both hands pointing to the twelve. Move the big hand until it points at the three. Help your child to see that it's moved a quarter of the way round the clock and introduce the term quarter past. Practise quarter past different hours using the clock face in the same way as you practised half past.

Stage 3
Again start with both hands pointing at the twelve but this time move the big hand round to the nine. Talk about the fact that it's still got a quarter of the way to go round before it's one o'clock and introduce the term quarter to. Use the clock face to practise quarter to different hours in the same way as you practised 'half past'.

Stage 4
Lastly, use the clock face to practise a mixture of half past, quarter to, quarter past and o'clock until your child can tell these times easily.

Moving On
Keep practising these times until your child can easily read them correctly. Then move on to step 3 or a different topic.

Step 3

Aims

1) To teach your child to read any possible time from a traditional clock.
2) To demonstrate the connection between traditional and digital clocks.

Essential Background Knowledge
Before starting this work your child should:
a) be able to tell the time using a digital clock
b) know that there are sixty minutes in each hour
c) be able to count in fives.

Tackling the Oral Work
Draw a clock face on a piece of paper and talk about the fact that the big hand takes sixty minutes to go right round it. Your conversation might sound like this:

YOU: If we wanted to, we could mark its position for each
        minute just as we mark the positions of the small hand.
        (*Write the numbers one to thirty round the first half of your
        picture like this*:)

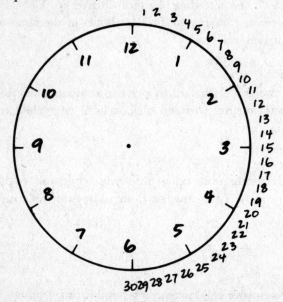

YOU: Oh dear! The further round we go, the messier it
        looks. And it's not easy to read either, is it?
CHILD: No.

YOU: I expect that's why people don't put those numbers in. They just work out how many minutes have gone past by looking at the numbers which mark the hours.

CHILD: How do they do that?

YOU: Look at how the numbers I've written fit round the clock. Five is beside the one, ten is beside the two, fifteen is beside the three, twenty is beside the four. Five, ten, fifteen, twenty. Does that remind you of anything?

CHILD: Counting in fives.

YOU: That's right. Now you can help me write in the other minutes numbers that match the hour numbers.
(*Together write the numbers in like this:*)

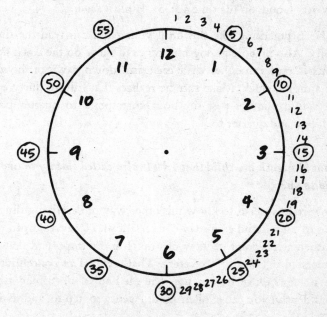

YOU: So if the little hand is pointing at the two and the big hand is pointing at the four like this (*set it up on your clock face*), how many minutes is it past two o'clock?

CHILD: Twenty.

YOU: Well done. And we call that time 2:20 (*write it down*), which is the same as on a digital clock. Now what time is this?
(*Set up 3:35 on the clockface.*)

CHILD: Umm.

YOU: Well, how many hours are there?

CHILD: Three.

YOU: Right. And how many minutes have gone by since three o'clock? If you can't remember, count round the clock face in fives.

CHILD: Five, ten, fifteen, twenty, twenty-five, thirty, thirty-five. That's it. There've been thirty-five minutes.

YOU: ·Good. So the time's 3:35. (*Write it down.*)

Keep practising like this until your child can read the time easily. Also practise giving him times to show on the clock face himself. You can either write each time down, say it or show it on a digital clock. Make sure he realizes that fifteen, thirty and forty-five minutes past the hour correspond to quarter past, half past and quarter to.

Should I teach my child that 1:40 is also called twenty to two, and so on?

He certainly needs to know this other way of describing time if he's to understand everyday conversations. However, from the mathematical point of view, it's much more important that he understands 1:40, 6:55, etcetera. That's why I've concentrated on it here. Once he can use that method of describing time confidently, you can explain about twenty to, ten to, and so on.

Moving On
Stay on this level until your child can read any time confidently and correctly from a traditional clock. Then move on to another topic.

USING THE TWENTY-FOUR-HOUR CLOCK AND TIMETABLES

Our custom of splitting the day into two twelve-hour periods can easily cause confusion. Adding am and pm to times helps but we frequently forget to do so or people don't notice when we do. Using the twenty-four-hour clock totally removes the problem which is why it's used in timetables and other situations where confusion might occur.

Understanding the twenty-four-hour clock involves adding and subtracting twelve. Unless your child can do this easily, he'll become so bogged down in the arithmetic that he'll find it difficult to follow your explanations. That's why we're starting this topic by looking at that particular skill.

Step 1

Aim
To practise adding and subtracting twelve.

Essential Background Knowledge
Before starting this work your child should be able to add and subtract numbers less than ten confidently.

Before You Start the Session
Write this exercise in your child's book:

1)	$12 + 3 =$	9)	$15 - 12 =$
2)	$12 + 6 =$	10)	$16 - 12 =$
3)	$12 + 8 =$	11)	$22 - 12 =$
4)	$12 + 4 =$	12)	$18 - 12 =$
5)	$12 + 10 =$	13)	$20 - 12 =$
6)	$12 + 12 =$	14)	$24 - 12 =$
7)	$12 + 2 =$	15)	$18 - 12 =$
8)	$12 + 11 =$	16)	$15 - 12 =$

To write more exercises, make up questions which involve adding twelve to any number between one and twelve or subtracting twelve from any number between thirteen and twenty-four.

Tackling the Exercise

If your child is worried because these numbers are larger than he's used to, encourage him to work out the answers by counting on or counting back as he normally would and let him use his fingers to help him if he wishes.

Moving On

Stay on this level until your child can add and subtract twelve confidently and accurately. Then move on to step 2.

Step 2

Aim

To introduce the principle of the twenty-four-hour clock.

Essential Background Knowledge

Before starting this work your child should:

a) understand the twelve-hour clock
b) know the numbers on a clock face tell you about hours
c) be able to add and subtract twelve confidently.

Tackling the Oral Work

Begin the session with a few counting exercises. Then tell your child the following story (adapted if necessary to fit in with his tastes). Jason Jones was going on the school holiday. The letter from his teacher told him to be at school on Saturday with his luggage, ready to get on the coach at seven o'clock. Saturday came and Jason was excited all day. He packed his bag, ate his tea and set off for school in the early evening. But there was no one there. The place was deserted. All he could find was a note pinned to the gatepost. It said: DEAR JASON, WE'RE SORRY WE MISSED YOU. WE WAITED AS LONG AS WE COULD BUT WE PROMISED TO BE AT THE CAMPSITE BY LUNCHTIME. SEE YOU NEXT WEEK.

Your child's almost sure to guess what's happened. Try making up some other stories together about confused times. Talk about the problem being caused by the fact that we count to twelve and then start again at one in the middle of the day. If we just kept counting on from twelve (saying thirteen, fourteen, fifteen . . .), life would be much less confusing as there would only be one two o'clock, one three o'clock and so on. This is such a sensible system that people really do use it to measure time. It's called the twenty-four-hour clock.

Now draw a clock face on a piece of paper and help your child write the numbers thirteen to twenty-three on it like this. Don't put twenty-four because midnight in the twenty-four-hour clock is 0:00.

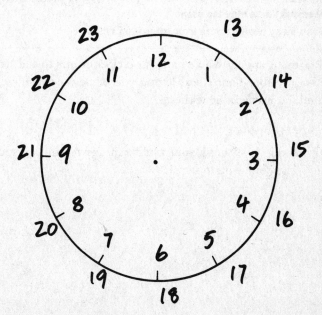

Look at the finished drawing together and talk about the fact that 2 pm is the same as 14:00 and 5 pm is the same as 17:00. Make sure your child notices that morning times are always twelve or less while afternoon times are always more than twelve.

Then ask him to find the difference between the morning time and the afternoon time for each pair of numbers. If necessary, help him to realize that the answer is always twelve hours. Point out that he can use that fact to help him change from one sort of time to the other.

REMEMBER
To change from the ordinary clock to the twenty-four-hour one:
   Morning times stay the same
   Add twelve hours to afternoon times

To change from the twenty-four-hour clock to the ordinary one:
   Morning times stay the same
   Take away twelve hours from afternoon times

Practise changing whole hour (or o'clock) times to and from the twenty-four-hour clock, letting your child use the drawing to find the answer if he wishes.

Moving On
Stay on this level until your child can answer the questions easily. Then move on to step 3.

Step 3

Aim
To practise changing times from the twelve-hour to the twenty-four-hour system and vice versa.

Essential Background Knowledge
Before starting this work your child should:
a) be able to read and write times in the form 11:50, 4:14, etcetera
b) be able to add and subtract twelve easily
c) understand the twenty-four-hour clock (see previous step).

Before You Start the Session
Write this exercise in your child's book:

1)	6 am =	9)	13:55 =
2)	5 pm =	10)	9:32 =
3)	14:00 =	11)	20:45 =
4)	18:00 =	12)	22:17 =
5)	1 pm =	13)	5:22 pm =
6)	3:45 pm =	14)	6:36 pm =
7)	2:30 am =	15)	14:30 =
8)	5:30 am =	16)	11:32 am =

To write more exercises, write times in either the ordinary or twenty-four-hour system and ask your child to change them to the other type. Include some morning times to remind him that these don't change.

Tackling the Exercise
The only difference between these questions and the ones in the previous step is that many of these times involve minutes. If your child adds twelve to the minutes instead of the hours (that is, 3:45pm = 3:57 instead of 15:45), encourage him to think about what the numbers mean and to realize

that, because the twelve is telling him about hours, he must add it to the number in the time which tells him about hours.

Moving On

Stay on this level until your child can answer this type of question easily and confidently. Then move on to another topic but continue to involve him when you meet the twenty-four-hour clock in real life.

TIMETABLES

Maths teachers love timetables so your child will be at an advantage at school if he can read one easily. He'll need to understand the twenty-four-hour clock before you start to practise at home unless you're careful and make sure everything you look up happens in the morning.

Choose straightforward timetables for buses, trains, planes or ferries (ones without masses of connections marked in). It's fun to plan imaginary journeys and even better if you can plan a real one.

CALCULATING WITH TIMES

Using timetables naturally leads on to working out how long a journey takes. Suppose the train leaves at 10:40 and arrives at 12:22. It's very tempting to subtract the starting time from the finishing time to find the interval between them. Unfortunately that's not as easy as it looks.

The problem is that there are sixty minutes in an hour not a hundred. Although 10:40 and 12:22 look very similar to ordinary decimal numbers, they're not. To subtract them involves adapting the standard techniques of arithmetic to base sixty. (Did I hear someone scream?)

I find it easier to break the problem into four stages which only use the skills we already have. For instance, to find the time between 10:40 and 12:22:

1) Work out how long it is from the starting time to the next whole hour (10:40 to 11:00 is twenty minutes).
2) Work out how many hours from then until the whole hour just before the finishing time (11:00 to 12:00 is one hour).
3) Work out how long it is from then until the finishing time (12:00 to 12:22 is twenty-two minutes).
4) Now add those three times together and you'll have the answer (20 minutes + 1 hour + 22 minutes is 1 hour 44 minutes).

That might sound horribly complicated but it's not really. Once your child has mastered the individual skills involved, he shouldn't find it too difficult.

Step 1

Aim
To practise adding periods of time together.

Essential Background Knowledge
Before starting this work your child should:
a) know there are sixty minutes in an hour
b) be able to add and subtract numbers less than sixty.

Before You Start the Session
Write this exercise in your child's book:

1) 30 mins + 20 mins =
2) 50 mins + 5 mins =
3) 15 mins + 30 mins =
4) 25 mins + 12 mins =
5) 20 mins + 40 mins =

6)   35 mins + 25 mins =
7)   15 mins + 45 mins =
8)   30 mins + 45 mins =
9)   1 hr 20 mins + 30 mins =
10)   1 hr 20 mins + 1 hr 10 mins =
11)   1 hr 30 mins + 40 mins =
12)   1 hr 30 mins + 2 hrs =

To write more exercises, make up questions asking your child to add together two or more periods of time.

Tackling the Exercise

When you first show your child the exercise, explain that the abbreviations mins and hrs stand for minutes and hours. (It's those lazy mathematicians saving themselves work again.) Make sure your child writes mins or hrs in the appropriate places in his answers.

When he finds the answer to question 5 is sixty minutes, you may need to remind him that that's an hour. Encourage him to write down his work like this:

20 mins + 40 mins = 60 mins = 1 hour.

When he reaches question 8, he'll find the answer is 75 mins. If necessary, help him to realize that this is the same as 1 hr 15 mins. Don't worry if he needs to use a pencil and paper to work this out.

Moving On

Stay on this level until your child can answer the questions confidently and accurately. Then move on to step 2.

Step 2

Aim

To practise finding how many minutes are left before the next hour.

Essential Background Knowledge

Before starting this work your child should:

a) know there are sixty minutes in an hour

b) be able to add and subtract numbers less than sixty

c) understand times written in the form 3:40, 11:55, etcetera.

Essential Background Knowledge

Before starting this work your child should:

a) know there are sixty minutes in an hour

b) be able to add and subtract numbers less than sixty

c) understand times written in the form 3:40, 11:55, etcetera.

Before You Start the Session

Write this exercise in your child's book:

1)	From 3:59 to 4:00 is	7)	From 14:05 to 15:00 is
2)	From 2:40 to 3:00 is	8)	From 20:45 to 21:00 is
3)	From 7:52 to 8:00 is	9)	From 11:02 to 12:00 is
4)	From 13:30 to 14:00 is	10)	From 9:51 to 10:00 is
5)	From 17:10 to 18:00 is	11)	From 8:55 to 9:00 is
6)	From 5:20 to 6:00 is	12)	From 6:50 to 7:00 is

To write more exercises, write similar questions asking your child how long it is from one time to the next whole hour.

Tackling the Exercise

If your child isn't sure how to tackle the first question, remind him that there are sixty minutes in an hour and help him to work out the answer. Continue to help him with each question until he's confident enough to work alone.

Moving On

Stay on this level until your child can answer the questions easily. Then move on to step 3.

Step 3

Aim
To enable your child to work out how long has passed between two times.

Essential Background Knowledge
Before starting this work your child should've worked through the previous two steps.

Before You Start the Session
Write this exercise in your child's book:

> 1) From 3:40 to 4:00 is
> 2) From 2:00 to 2:35 is
> 3) From 5:00 to 6:17 is
> 4) From 2:00 to 4:10 is
> 5) From 2:40 to 3:20 is
> 6) From 5:15 to 6:10 is
> 7) From 2:45 to 3:25 is
> 8) From 3:45 to 7:00 is
> 9) From 3:30 to 6:10 is
> 10) From 3:20 to 7:00 is

To write more exercises, make up similar questions including some using times written in the twenty-four-hour system.

Tackling the Exercise
The questions in this exercise gradually become more complicated to introduce your child gently to working out the period between two times (often called elapsed time). He has already practised all the skills he needs in the earlier steps so he only needs to gain confidence in applying them. If he's not sure what to do, encourage him to break the task into the steps I described at the beginning of this section and to write his working down like this:

7) From 2:45 to 3:25 is 15 mins + 25 mins = 40 mins
8) From 3:45 to 7:00 is 15 mins + 3 hrs = 3 hrs 15 mins
9) From 3:30 to 6:10 is 30 mins + 2 hrs + 10 mins = 2 hrs 40 mins

Moving On
Stay on this level until your child can answer the questions easily and confidently. Then move on to any other topic.

22 / Fractions

Decimal currency and the introduction of calculators have changed the way fractions are taught in schools. Just as in real life, the emphasis is on decimals. Although your child still needs to understand ordinary fractions like $\frac{1}{2}$ and $\frac{1}{4}$ they play a much smaller role in arithmetic than they did years ago. That's why I've not included addition, subtraction, multiplication and division of fractions as your child will only meet these topics later in her school career.

Visualizing Fractions

The best way to help your child understand what fractions mean is to encourage her to think about cutting up a round cake. Using a real cake makes the activity more enjoyable but it's expensive to keep doing so (not to mention all those calories). Fortunately, drawing circles and dividing them into sections works equally well.

INTRODUCING FRACTIONS

Step 1

Aim
To introduce the basic concept of fractions.

Essential Background Knowledge
None required.

Tackling the Topic

This basic introductory work is best done informally. Involve your child in situations where you're sharing out items – cooking and serving food are particularly useful activities. Use these opportunities to introduce your child to the language of fractions, emphasizing the relationship between the number of pieces you've divided something into and the name of each piece. For instance, you might say 'I'll cut the sandwich into two and we'll have half each.'

While you're using fractions in a practical way, try to introduce the following ideas:

a) The size of a fraction depends on the size of the whole. So half an elephant is bigger than half a mouse.

b) Some fractions are larger than others. If you cut a cake into quarters, the pieces will be bigger than if you'd cut it into sixths.

c) Some fractions can be made from other fractions. For instance, if you cut a cake into quarters and then cut each piece in half, you've cut it into eighths. The opposite is true as well: two eighths of the same size cake make one quarter.

Moving On

Stay on this level until your child can talk confidently about fractions and understands the meaning of half, quarter, third, sixth and eighth. Then move on to step 2.

Step 2

Aim

To introduce the written notation for fractions.

Essential Background Knowledge

Before starting this work your child should have a basic understanding of fractions.

Before You Start the Session
Write this exercise in your child's book:

1) If you split something into 2 pieces, each piece is called
2) If you split something into 3 pieces, each piece is called
3) If you split something into 4 pieces, each piece is called
4) If you split something into 5 pieces, each piece is called
5) If you split something into 6 pieces, each piece is called
6) If you split something into 8 pieces, each piece is called
7) If you split something into 10 pieces, each piece is called
8) If you split something into 100 pieces, each piece is called

What fraction is shaded?

9)

12)

10)

13)

11)

14)

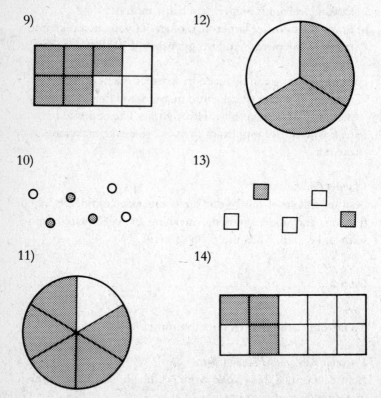

To write more exercises, draw shapes split into equal numbers of pieces or groups of identical shapes. For some questions, shade part of the picture and ask your child to write down which fraction is shaded. For the others, write a fraction beside your drawing and ask your child to colour in that fraction of the picture.

Tackling the Exercise

When you've finished the oral part of the session, look at the first question together. Your child will know that the answer is a half but explain that mathematicians don't usually write the word: it's too much like hard work. Instead they write numbers one on top of the other like this: $\frac{1}{2}$. It's like a secret code which means one of the pieces you get when you split something into two. Give her as much help as she needs to tackle the other similar questions and check each time that she understands the code.

The second part of the exercise involves fractions whose top number is greater than one. If she finds them difficult, remind her that the bottom number tells us how many pieces something was split into and the top number tells us how many pieces we have. So in question 9, where five of the eight pieces are shaded, the fraction is $\frac{5}{8}$. Give her as much help as she needs until she's confident enough to work alone.

Moving On

Stay on this level until your child can identify and write fractions easily. Then move on to another topic.

CALCULATING A FRACTION OF A NUMBER

Step 1

Aim

To develop a method of finding a fraction of a number.

Essential Background Knowledge
Before starting this work your child should:
a) understand what fractions are and how to write them
b) be able to multiply and divide by numbers no larger than
   ten.

Before You Start the Session
Write this exercise in your child's book:

1)	$\frac{1}{2}$ of 6 is	7)	$\frac{1}{4}$ of 16 is
2)	$\frac{1}{4}$ of 8 is	8)	$\frac{1}{5}$ of 45 is
3)	$\frac{1}{3}$ of 9 is	9)	$\frac{1}{3}$ of 15 is
4)	$\frac{1}{2}$ of 18 is	10)	$\frac{1}{10}$ of 50 is
5)	$\frac{1}{5}$ of 15 is	11)	$\frac{1}{4}$ of 20 is
6)	$\frac{1}{10}$ of 30 is	12)	$\frac{1}{2}$ of 14 is

To write more exercises, make up similar questions involving fractions with one as their top number. In each question, make sure that the bottom number of the fraction will divide exactly into the whole number and concentrate on the tables your child knows well.

Tackling the Exercise
If she's not sure what to do, encourage your child to use coins to help her see what is happening. For instance, for question 1, she can take six pennies, divide them into two equal piles and count how many are in one pile. As she works through the questions, help her to realize that this is another way of asking her to divide one number by another.

Moving On
Stay on this level until your child can answer the questions confidently and accurately without using coins. Then move on to step 2 or another topic.

Step 2

Aim
To show the connection between multiplication, division and finding a fraction of a number.

Essential Background Knowledge
Don't start this work until your child has successfully completed the previous step.

Before You Start the Session
Write this exercise in your child's book:

1) $\frac{1}{2} \times 2 =$ 7) $\frac{1}{2} \times 10 =$

2) $\frac{1}{2} \times 4 =$ 8) $\frac{1}{5} \times 25 =$

3) $\frac{1}{4} \times 4 =$ 9) $\frac{1}{6} \times 12 =$

4) $\frac{1}{4} \times 8 =$ 10) $\frac{1}{4} \times 16 =$

5) $\frac{1}{3} \times 3 =$ 11) $\frac{1}{5} \times 35 =$

6) $\frac{1}{3} \times 9 =$ 12) $\frac{1}{2} \times 20 =$

To write more exercises, make up similar questions involving fractions with one as their top number. Make sure the bottom number of the fraction will divide exactly into the whole number.

Tackling the Exercise
If your child isn't sure how to tackle these questions, remind her that multiplication is successive addition. 5×2 means five lots of two added together and 8×2 means eight lots of two, so $\frac{1}{2} \times 2$ means half a lot of two. Illustrate this with piles of coins to help her see that $\frac{1}{2} \times 2$ is just another way of writing $\frac{1}{2}$ of 2.

Many people find this a very difficult idea to grasp so don't worry if your child does too. Be prepared to explain each question in this way until she's confident enough to work alone.

Once she can cope happily with questions written in this way (which may take more than one session), talk to her about the fact that she's using division to find the answers although the questions are about multiplication. This means you've found yet another way to write division:

$$\times \tfrac{1}{2} \text{ means the same as } \div 2$$
$$\times \tfrac{1}{3} \text{ means the same as } \div 3 \text{ and so on.}$$

This may seem a fairly trivial fact at the moment but it will be very useful in more advanced work.

Moving On
Stay on this level until your child can answer the questions confidently and accurately. Then move on to step 3 or another topic.

Step 3

Aim
To practise multiplying a whole number by a fraction whose top number is greater than one.

Essential Background Knowledge
Don't start this work until your child has successfully completed steps 1 and 2.

Before You Start the Session
Write this exercise in your child's book:

1)	$\tfrac{1}{3} \times 6 =$	6)	$\tfrac{3}{5} \times 20 =$
2)	$\tfrac{2}{3} \times 6 =$	7)	$\tfrac{4}{10} \times 100 =$
3)	$\tfrac{1}{5} \times 10 =$	8)	$\tfrac{2}{3} \times 9 =$
4)	$\tfrac{3}{5} \times 10 =$	9)	$\tfrac{3}{4} \times 20 =$
5)	$\tfrac{1}{4} \times 12 =$	10)	$\tfrac{2}{3} \times 6 =$

To write more exercises, make up similar questions where the top number of the fraction is smaller than the bottom number but greater than one and the bottom number divides exactly into the whole number.

Tackling the Exercise

If your child isn't sure how to tackle the second question, remind her that she's just found one third of six in question 1. She can use that answer to help her find this one because two thirds is twice as big as one third. Encourage her to use the same approach throughout the exercise, so for question 6 she can first find one fifth of twenty and then work out three fifths.

Moving On

Stay on this level until your child can answer the questions confidently and accurately with only occasional mistakes. Then move on to another topic.

THE CONNECTION BETWEEN DIVISION AND FRACTIONS

Aim

To introduce the idea that $\frac{4}{5}$ means the same as $4 \div 5$.

Essential Background Knowledge

Before starting this work your child should:
a) be able to read and write fractions
b) be able to multiply and divide by numbers less than ten.

Before You Start the Session

Write this exercise in your child's book:

$$\begin{array}{lll} 1) & 8 \div 4 = & \text{and} & 2 = \frac{}{4} \\ & \text{so } 8 \div 4 = \end{array}$$

2) $6 \div 2 =$ and $3 = \frac{}{2}$
    so $6 \div 2 =$

3) $10 \div 5 =$ and $2 = \frac{}{5}$
    so $10 \div 2 =$

4) $12 \div 2 =$ and $6 = \frac{}{2}$
    so $12 \div 2 =$

5) $20 \div 5 =$ and $4 = \frac{}{5}$
    so $20 \div 5 =$

6) $\frac{14}{7} =$ 9) $\frac{25}{5} =$

7) $\frac{9}{3} =$ 10) $\frac{8}{2} =$

8) $\frac{16}{2} =$

To write more exercises, write down fractions where the bottom number is smaller than the top one and divides into it exactly.

Tackling the Exercise

Show your child the exercise and ask her to fill in the gaps in the first question. She'll manage the first part easily but she may not be sure how to manage the second. If necessary, help her to see how many quarters there are in two by drawing two identical circles and asking her to divide each one into four. Reassure her that it's all right for a fraction to have the top number larger than the bottom number when you are talking about dividing up more than one thing.

Her answers should look like this:

$$8 \div 4 = 2 \qquad \text{and} \qquad 2 = \tfrac{8}{4}.$$

Point out that $8 \div 4$ and $\frac{8}{4}$ are both equal to two and help her to realize that this means they must be equal to each other. Finish off the first question by writing:

$$\text{so } 8 \div 4 = \tfrac{8}{4}$$

Let her work through the next four questions in the same way, giving her as much help as she needs. When she's finished question 5, ask her to look back at her answers and help her to realize that she's found yet another way of writing down division. Then let her use her new knowledge to answer the remaining questions by dividing the top number of the fraction by the bottom one.

REMEMBER

It's very important that your child remembers this connection between division and fractions. She'll use it a great deal in the future.

Moving on
Stay on this level until your child can confidently answer division questions written in the form of a fraction. Then move on to another topic.

EQUIVALENT FRACTIONS

During your informal work together on fractions, your child will have noticed that some fractions are the same size. For instance, you get the same portion of cake whether you have one quarter or two eighths. Mathematicians describe this by saying one quarter and two eighths are equivalent fractions.

Step 1

Aim
To introduce the idea of equivalent fractions.

Essential Background Knowledge
Before starting this work your child should:
a) know what fractions are and how they are written
b) be able to multiply and divide by numbers no larger than ten.

Equipment:
You'll need a knife and a cake (or other food suitable for cutting into portions).

Before You Start the Session
Write this exercise in your child's book:

1) $\frac{1}{2} = \frac{}{4}$ 6) $\frac{1}{2} = \frac{}{100}$

2) $\frac{1}{2} = \frac{}{6}$ 7) $\frac{1}{6} = \frac{}{12}$

3) $\frac{1}{2} = \frac{}{10}$ 8) $\frac{1}{4} = \frac{}{12}$

4) $\frac{1}{4} = \frac{}{8}$ 9) $\frac{1}{4} = \frac{}{20}$

5) $\frac{1}{10} = \frac{}{100}$ 10) $\frac{1}{3} = \frac{}{6}$

To write more exercises, make up similar questions where the bottom number of the first fraction will divide exactly into the bottom number of the second one. The top number of the first fraction should always be one.

Tackling the Topic
After you've finished the oral work, ask your child to cut the cake into quarters. From then on, your conversation might sound like this:

YOU: Cut one of the quarters into two. (*Child does so.*) Now what fraction of the whole cake is each of the pieces you've just made?

CHILD: Ummm?

YOU: Well, if you cut the whole cake into pieces that size, how many would you have?

CHILD: Eight. Oh, so they're all eighths.

YOU: That's right. And how many of those eighths pushed together make a quarter?

CHILD: Two.

YOU: Good. So two eighths means the same as one quarter. Now cut one of the other quarters into three. (*Child does so.*) What fraction of the whole cake is one of those pieces?

CHILD: A twelfth?

YOU: Good. You're really getting the idea now. So how many twelfths are the same as one quarter?

CHILD: Three.

Continue in a similar way asking your child to cut the next quarter into four to make sixteenths. If the cake isn't very big, you may be better just talking about this or drawing a picture.

Now show your child the exercise while you both eat some cake. Explain that you want her to fill in the missing numbers to make the pairs of fractions the same size.

The work you've just done may help her realize how to work out the answers. If not, encourage her to think about cutting up a cake again. Your conversation about question 2 might sound like this:

YOU: How many pieces must you cut a cake into to make sixths?

CHILD: Six.

YOU: And how many of those pieces would you have to push together to make half a cake?

CHILD: I'm not sure.

YOU: Well, let's draw a picture so we can see what's happening. (*Draw a circle divided into six.*)

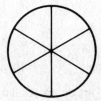

CHILD: Three of them make a half.

YOU: That's right. That's because two threes make six. Put the answer in and try the next one.

Continue in this way with each question until your child's confident enough to work alone. Stress each time that she can find the answer by asking herself what number she needs to multiply the bottom number of the first fraction by in order to get the second.

Moving On
Stay on this level until your child can answer the questions confidently without drawing pictures. Then move on to step 2.

Step 2

Aim
To extend the idea of equivalent fractions to fractions whose top number is greater than one.

Essential Background Knowledge
Don't start this work until your child has completed the previous step.

Before You Start the Session
Write this exercise in your child's book:

1) $\frac{1}{2} = \frac{}{10}$ 6) $\frac{2}{3} = \frac{}{12}$

2) $\frac{2}{3} = \frac{}{6}$ 7) $\frac{3}{4} = \frac{}{20}$

3) $\frac{3}{4} = \frac{}{8}$ 8) $\frac{7}{10} = \frac{}{100}$

4) $\frac{3}{10} = \frac{}{100}$ 9) $\frac{2}{3} = \frac{}{15}$

5) $\frac{5}{6} = \frac{}{12}$ 10) $\frac{5}{10} = \frac{}{20}$

To write more exercises, make up similar questions where the bottom number of the first fraction divides exactly into the bottom number of the second fraction. The top number of the first fraction can be larger than one but it should always be smaller than the bottom number.

Tackling the Exercise

When you show your child the exercise, point out that some of the fractions have a top number larger than one and remind her that this number tells her how many pieces she has. Be prepared to work with her if she isn't sure what to do. Your conversation might sound like this:

YOU: Let's draw a cake and divide it into thirds. (*Draw a picture.*) How many sixths can we make out of each of those thirds?

CHILD: Two.

YOU: Good. So if we cut two of the thirds into sixths like this, how many sixths have we got?

CHILD: Four?

YOU: That's right. Two thirds are twice as big as one third so they contain twice as many sixths.

Keep helping your child in this way until she realizes that she needs to multiply the top and the bottom of the fraction by the same number. Then gradually reduce your help as she gains confidence.

Moving On

Stay on this level until your child can answer the questions accurately and confidently without drawing pictures. Then move on to step 3.

Step 3

Aim

To practise changing one fraction into another with a smaller bottom number. (This process is often called cancelling.)

Essential Background Knowledge

Don't start this work with your child until she's successfully completed the previous two steps.

Before You Start the Session

Write this exercise in your child's book:

1) $\frac{2}{4} = \frac{}{2}$ 6) $\frac{9}{12} = \frac{}{4}$

2) $\frac{6}{8} = \frac{}{4}$ 7) $\frac{6}{9} = \frac{}{3}$

3) $\frac{30}{100} = \frac{}{10}$ 8) $\frac{18}{27} = \frac{}{9} = \frac{}{3}$

4) $\frac{12}{18} = \frac{}{6}$ 9) $\frac{50}{100} = \frac{}{10} = \frac{}{2}$

5) $\frac{20}{25} = \frac{}{5}$ 10) $\frac{6}{12} = \frac{}{2}$

To write more exercises, make up similar questions where the top and bottom of the first fraction can both be divided by the same number. The second fraction is the one you would find by actually doing that division but leave a space instead of writing the top number.

Tackling the Exercise

If necessary, work with your child and draw pictures to explain what you're doing (as you did for the previous step). Help her to realize that she needs to divide the top and bottom numbers of the fraction by the same number to find the answer.

REMEMBER

If you multiply or divide the top and bottom numbers of a fraction by the same number, you'll make a new fraction which is the same size as the old one.

Moving On
Stay on this level until your child can answer the questions confidently and well. Then move on to another topic.

Putting Fractions in Their Lowest Terms

This means changing a fraction into an equivalent one with the smallest possible bottom number. The maths involved is identical to that covered in step 3 except your child has to choose the new bottom number herself. If you want her to practise this process because she's doing it at school, write questions similar to those in step 3 but without telling her which bottom number to use. Don't worry if she takes more than one attempt to reach the final answer. For instance, both these examples are equally correct

$$\cdot \frac{6}{24} = \frac{3}{12} = \frac{1}{4}$$
$$\frac{6}{24} = \frac{1}{4}.$$

WRITING ONE NUMBER AS A FRACTION OF ANOTHER

Essential Background Knowledge
Before starting this work your child should know what fractions are and be able to write them.

Before You Start the Session
Write this exercise in your child's book, leaving space for two lines of writing between each question:

1) 3 as a fraction of 5
2) 7 as a fraction of 10
3) 3 as a fraction of 5
4) 46 as a fraction of 100
5) 7 as a fraction of 15
6) 22 as a fraction of 25
7) 48 as a fraction of 200
8) 93 as a fraction of 149
9) 65 as a fraction of 261
10) 25 as a fraction of 75
11) 100 as a fraction of 152
12) 3 as a fraction of 4

To write more exercises, make up questions asking your child to write one number as a fraction of another larger one.

Tackling the Exercise
If your child isn't sure what to do, you'll need to work with her. Your conversation about question 1 might sound like this:

YOU: So what I want you to do is to tell me what fraction of five is three.

CHILD: I don't know how to do that.

YOU: I bet you can do it if we think of something easier first.

CHILD: Like what?

YOU: Suppose we've got five coins and we divide them into piles with one in each pile. (*Lay five coins on the table*.) How many piles have we got?

CHILD: Five.

YOU: Right. So what fraction of five is one?

CHILD: One fifth?

YOU: Very good. Let's write that down before we forget. (*Write: 1 is $\frac{1}{5}$ of 5 under question 1.*) Now let's look at those coins again. If I want three of them, how many of the piles must I take?

CHILD: Three.

YOU: Now each of those piles is one fifth of five. So if I want three, how many fifths must I take?

CHILD: Three.

YOU: So if I take three, what fraction of five have I taken?

CHILD (*doubtfully*): Three fifths?

YOU: Very good. I was sure you'd be able to do it. Let's write down the answer. (*Write: so 3 is $\frac{3}{5}$ of 5 under your previous statement.*)

Keep working with your child in this way, gradually letting her take over once she gains confidence.

Moving On
Stay on this level until your child can answer the questions
easily and confidently. Then move on to another topic.

23 / Decimals

Calculations can become very complicated when they involve fractions written in the conventional way as one number on top of another. To make life easier, mathematicians have developed another way of writing fractions which we call decimals. They are a natural extension of place value so we can use the same methods to add, subtract, multiply and divide them as we use for whole numbers.

INTRODUCING DECIMALS

There's nothing magical or mysterious about decimals. They're just an alternatve way of writing tenths, hundredths, thousandths, etcetera. The decimal point is only there to tell us where the whole numbers end and the fractions begin. Once your child understands this, he should gradually lose any fear he may have developed of this topic from meeting it unsuccessfully in the past.

Step 1

Aim
To introduce the use of the decimal point.

Essential Background Knowledge
Before starting this work your child should have a basic understanding of fractions.

Equipment

You'll need some adverts or labels which use decimals to show prices greater than £1 or quantities measured in litres, kilos or metres.

Tackling the Oral Work

Start the oral session with some straightforward counting work. Then give your child £1 coin, six 10ps and four pennies, and talk about the way we write prices. Your conversation might sound like this:

YOU: If I changed all those coins into pennies, how many would I have?

CHILD: 164.

YOU: Right. So those coins are worth 164p. (*Write 164p.*) Is that how they write the price in a shop when something costs more than a pound?

CHILD: No. They use pounds and dots.

YOU: That's right. They'd write 164 pence as one pound sixty-four. (*Write £1·64.*) That dot's got a special name. It's called a decimal point.

Break off here to look at the examples you've found where measurements or prices are written using decimals. As you talk about them together, help your child to understand that:

a) The numbers after the decimal point are similar to fractions as they tell us about something smaller than one.

b) 2·53 is larger than two and smaller than three; 1·2 is larger than one and smaller than two, etcetera.

c) We usually say three point five two when we mean the number 3·52. It's only when we talk about money that we say three fifty-two.

Moving On
Stay on this level until your child seems comfortable with decimals and has absorbed the above three points. Then move on to step 2 or another topic.

Step 2

Aim
To extend place value to include decimals.

Essential Background Knowledge
Before starting this work your child should:
a) understand place value
b) have a basic understanding of fractions
c) know that the numbers to the right of the decimal point tell you about something smaller than one.

Tackling the Oral Work
Write down 7352 and ask your child to read the number aloud. If he can't do this, stop here and revise place value (chapter 13) before you go any further.

If he can read it, talk to him about what each of the individual numbers mean. Your conversation might sound like this:

YOU: So the seven tells us about the thousands.
      (*Write Th above the seven.*)
      The three tells us about the hundreds.
      (*Write H above the three.*)
      The five tells us about the tens.
      (*Write T above the five.*)
      And the two tells us about the ones.
      (*Write 1 above the two.*)

Th H T 1
7 3 5 2

CHILD: My teacher used to write letters like that to help us but we don't need them now.

YOU: Don't worry. I'm only putting them in this time to help us think about something else. Suppose we've got a tiny bit more than 7352. Suppose we've got 7352·49. (*Write in the ·49.*)

$$\text{Th H T 1}$$
$$7\ 3\ 5\ 2\ \cdot\ 4\ 9$$

What do you think the four is telling us about?

CHILD: Umm?

YOU: Well, what would it be telling us about if this number was money?

CHILD: 10ps.

YOU: Right. And how many 10ps make £1?

CHILD: Ten.

YOU: So what fraction of £1 is 10p?

CHILD: One tenth.

YOU: Good. So the four is telling us about tenths. And that fits in with what the other numbers tell us about too.

CHILD: Does it?

YOU: Yes, because ten hundreds make one thousand, ten tens make a hundred, ten ones make ten and ten tenths make one.

$$\text{Th H T 1}\ \ ^{1}/_{10}$$
$$7\ 3\ 5\ 2\ \cdot\ 4\ 9$$

Now what does that nine tell us about?

CHILD: If it was money, it would mean pennies and ten pennies make 10p, so that fits too.

YOU: Very good. I'm delighted at how quickly you are
        understanding this. Now how many pennies are there
        in £1?

CHILD: A hundred.

YOU: So what fraction of £1 is a penny?

CHILD: One hundredth.

YOU: Great. So the nine is telling us about hundredths and
        that fits the pattern too because ten hundredths make
        one tenth.

$$Th \ H \ T \ 1 \ \tfrac{1}{10} \ \tfrac{1}{100}$$
$$7 \ 3 \ 5 \ 2 \cdot 4 \ 9$$

To save space, I've made my imaginary child catch on to this
idea very quickly. Don't worry if you have to explain it
several times using different numbers before your child
understands.

Moving On

Stay on this level until your child knows that the first two
numbers after the decimal point tell us about tenths and
hundredths. Then move on to step 3 or another topic.

Step 3

Aim

To practise writing decimal numbers.

Equipment

You'll need some price tickets made from pieces of paper or
card. Mark six with the following prices: £1·43, £2·72, £1·04,
£1·08, £1·80, £1·35. Leave the rest blank.

Tackling the Oral Work

Start the session with some basic counting work. Then give your child the first price card and ask him to give you that amount of money. If you wish, you can make the activity more interesting by making up a story about it.

Continue doing this with the other price cards. When you reach £1·04 and £1·08, point out how important that zero is. It's there to make sure we know the four and the eight are telling us about pennies (or hundredths) not 10ps (or tenths).

When you've used all the cards, play the game the other way by giving your child an amount of money and asking him to write a price ticket to match it. Make the first few amounts involve pounds, 10ps and pennies. When you're sure he can cope with these, give him some without any 10ps (for example, £1·03) but be ready to remind him to put in the zero if he forgets.

Possible Further Work

You can also practise reading and writing decimals while you're measuring lengths in metres, volumes of liquids in litres or weights in kilograms. Before starting to use the third decimal place, talk about place value again to help your child see that it tells us about thousandths (the fraction we get if we split one hundredth into ten).

Moving On

Stay on this level until your child can read and write decimals confidently and correctly. You can then move on to using decimals in calculations or another topic.

ARITHMETIC WITH DECIMALS

Once your child can read and write decimals easily, you can start to introduce them into your written work. Your child should cope with this without much trouble as adding, subtracting, multiplying and dividing decimals use the same techniques he already knows for whole numbers.

Introduce decimals into arithmetic in the following order:

- addition without carrying
- subtraction without decomposition or borrowing
- addition with carrying
- subtraction with decomposition or borrowing
- multiplication of a decimal number by a whole number
- division of a decimal number by a whole number
- multiplication and division by ten, a hundred and a thousand
- multiplying by a decimal
- dividing by a decimal.

However, always use whole numbers to introduce new skills. Only use decimals in questions when you're sure your child can confidently answer similar ones with whole numbers.

If your child runs into problems, you can adapt the explanations in Section 2 to fit the new situation, provided you remember that ten hundredths make one tenth and ten tenths make one. You'll also find some extra ideas on multiplication and division later in this chapter.

Remember to encourage your child to work neatly and set him a good example yourself when you write the exercises. He's sure to make mistakes unless all the numbers in a sum are written with the decimal points underneath each other like this:

$$
\begin{array}{r}
76 \cdot 5 \\
+\quad 8 \cdot 6 \\
+\quad 0 \cdot 05 \\
\hline
85 \cdot 15 \\
11
\end{array}
$$

Tackling Division

Once your child understands decimals, he no longer needs always to write a remainder when a number doesn't divide exactly. Instead he can keep working as if there were as many zeros as he needs after the decimal point.

So instead of

$$\overset{\displaystyle 9\ \ \text{rem}3}{4\overline{)39}}$$

he can write

$$\overset{\displaystyle 9 \cdot 7\,5}{4\overline{)39 \cdot {}^{3}0{}^{2}0}}$$

and $4{\cdot}5 \div 2$ becomes

$$\overset{\displaystyle 2 \cdot 2\,5}{2\overline{)4 \cdot 5'0}}$$

MULTIPLYING AND DIVIDING BY TEN, A HUNDRED AND A THOUSAND

Before You Start

Read the advice in chapter 25 on introducing multiplication by ten and a hundred.

Multiplication

When your child can confidently multiply decimal numbers by any whole number for which he knows the tables, give him an exercise which just practises multiplying by ten. Make some of the questions involve multiplying whole numbers and some of them involve decimals.

When he's finished the exercise successfully, talk about the answers. Help him to see that, in each question, each figure in the original number has moved one place to the left: the hundredths have become tenths, the tenths ones, the ones tens, the tens hundreds, etcetera. For whole numbers, this process leaves a space in the ones column, so we put a zero there. Let him practise using this fact to answer questions before you move on to other work.

You can repeat this process to help your child discover that multiplying by a hundred moves each figure two places to the left and multiplying by a thousand moves them three places to the left. (Be ready to help him with the exercises if he's not sure how to carry hundreds and thousands.)

Division

When your child can confidently divide decimal numbers by whole numbers no larger than nine, give him an exercise which only involves dividing by ten. When he's completed it successfully, talk about the answers.

Help him to see that each figure in the original number has moved one place to the right to make the answer. The hundreds have become tens, tens have become ones, the ones have become tenths and the tenths have become hundredths. Let him practise using this fact to divide by ten before you move on to other work.

You can repeat this process to help him discover that dividing by a hundred moves each figure two places to the right and that dividing by a thousand moves each figure three places to the right. In each case, don't worry if he needs considerable help answering the exercise. He won't need to work out answers in that way again: in future he'll be able to do it quickly by moving the figures the correct number of places to the right.

REMEMBER
It's the numbers that move, not the decimal point.

MULTIPLYING BY A DECIMAL

The ordinary technique for multiplying by whole numbers runs into trouble with questions like 176×0.5 or 24.5×0.3. To show your child how to multiply by a decimal, work through the following two steps.

Essential Background Knowledge
Before starting this work your child should:

a) be able to multiply and divide decimal numbers by ten, a hundred and a thousand
b) be able to multiply a decimal by a whole number.

Step 1

Aim
To show your child that any decimal number can be written as a whole number divided by ten, a hundred, a thousand, etcetera.

Before You Start the Session
Write this exercise in your child's book:

1)	$0.5 =$	$\div\ 10$		9)	$17.4 =$	$\div$
2)	$3.7 =$	$\div\ 10$		10)	$3.76 =$	$\div$
3)	$14.9 =$	$\div\ 10$		11)	$45.7 =$	$\div$
4)	$0.45 =$	$\div\ 100$		12)	$0.961 =$	$\div$
5)	$5.32 =$	$\div\ 100$		13)	$0.62 =$	$\div$
6)	$65.45 =$	$\div\ 100$		14)	$9.4 =$	$\div$
7)	$0.123 =$	$\div\ 1000$		15)	$3.7 =$	$\div$
8)	$7.625 =$	$\div\ 1000$		16)	$0.9 =$	$\div$

Tackling the Exercise
When you show your child the exercise, explain that you want
him to fill in the gaps. Work with him, if necessary, and help
him to see that the answers should look like this:

$$1) \quad 0·5 = 5 ÷ 10$$
$$4) \quad 0·45 = 45 ÷ 100$$
$$7) \quad 0·123 = 123 ÷ 1000$$

Moving On
Keep practising this process until your child can manage it
without difficulty. Then move on to the next step.

Step 2

Aim
To introduce multiplying by a decimal.

Before You Start the Session
Write this exercise in your child's book, leaving at least two
lines between the questions:

1)	$34 × 0·2 =$	7)	$86 × 0·5 =$
2)	$13 × 0·3 =$	8)	$149 × 0·2 =$
3)	$176 × 0·2 =$	9)	$25 × 0·8 =$
4)	$359 × 0·1 =$	10)	$15 × 0·9 =$
5)	$17 × 0·5 =$	11)	$32 × 0·7 =$
6)	$29 × 0·3 =$	12)	$396 × 0·1 =$

To write more exercises, make up questions asking your child to
multiply any number by 0·1, 0·2, 0·3, 0·4, 0·5, 0·6, 0·7, 0·8 or
0·9. Don't ask him to multiply by any other decimal numbers
unless he can already confidently tackle long multiplication.

Tackling the Exercise

Work the first question with your child to show him what to do. Explain that the fact that 0·2 is the same as 2 ÷ 10 is going to help him. Write:

$$34 \times 0{\cdot}2 = 34 \times 2 \div 10$$

Ask him to multiply 34 by 2. Write down his answer so the question now looks like this:

$$34 \times 0{\cdot}2 = 34 \times 2 \div 10$$
$$= 68 \div 10 =$$

When he's worked out that the final answer is 6·8, let him use a calculator to check if he's right. Continue to work each question with him in this way until he's confident enough to work alone.

Moving On

Stay on this level until your child can confidently multiply by a decimal with only occasional mistakes. Then move on to another topic.

DIVIDING BY A DECIMAL

Your child can divide by a decimal quite easily provided he knows that if he multiplies both numbers in a division question by ten, the answer to the division will still be the same. To introduce this idea, let him use a calculator to work out these questions

$$0{\cdot}5 \quad \div \; 0{\cdot}04 =$$
$$5 \quad \div \; 0{\cdot}4 =$$
$$50 \quad \div \; 4 =$$
$$500 \quad \div \; 40 =$$
$$5000 \div 400 =$$

When he's found that they all have the same answer, help him to see that each question is the same as the one before except that both numbers have been multiplied by ten. He can experiment with the calculator to see if the same is true for other division questions.

Once he understands this idea, you can show him how to use it to change a question which involves dividing by a decimal into one where he has to divide by a whole number. For instance:

$$68 \div 0.2 = 680 \div 2 = 340$$

$$4.5 \div 0.09 = 450 \div 9 = 50$$

Make sure the questions will only result in him needing to divide by a whole number less than ten. Once he can cope with these, only move on to harder questions if he's already very confident with long division.

CHANGING A DECIMAL INTO A FRACTION

Essential Background Knowledge
Before starting this work your child should:
a) be able to read and write decimals
b) be able to read and write fractions.

Before You Start the Session
Write this exercise in your child's book:

1)	$0.1 =$	7)	$0.001 =$
2)	$0.2 =$	8)	$0.002 =$
3)	$0.7 =$	9)	$0.004 =$
4)	$0.01 =$	10)	$0.45 =$
5)	$0.02 =$	11)	$0.76 =$
6)	$0.06 =$	12)	$0.035 =$

13) $0 \cdot 062 =$ 17) $0 \cdot 80 =$
14) $0 \cdot 397 =$ 18) $0 \cdot 08 =$
15) $0 \cdot 4 =$ 19) $0 \cdot 963 =$
16) $0 \cdot 9 =$ 20) $0 \cdot 9 =$

To write more exercises, write down decimal numbers which are smaller than one and ask your child to change them into fractions.

Tackling the Exercise
The first nine questions are straightforward but be prepared to work with your child if necessary. His answers should look like this:

$$1) \quad 0.1 = \tfrac{1}{10}$$

$$4) \quad 0.01 = \tfrac{1}{100}$$

When he reaches question 10, he'll find there are four tenths and five hundredths. You can help him realize that this is the same as forty-five hundredths by encouraging him to think how many pennies there are in £0·45. You can also remind him that one tenth is the same as ten hundredths.

Moving On
Stay on this level until your child can confidently and accurately change any decimal number less than one into a fraction. Then move on to another topic.

CHANGING A FRACTION INTO A DECIMAL

Essential Background Knowledge
Before starting this work your child should:

a) be able to read and write fractions
b) be able to read and write decimals
c) know that a fraction is another way of writing division.

Before You Start the Session

Write this exercise in your child's book:

1)	$\frac{1}{10} =$	9)	$\frac{7}{20} =$
2)	$\frac{1}{2} =$	10)	$\frac{5}{8} =$
3)	$\frac{1}{4} =$	11)	$\frac{9}{16} =$
4)	$\frac{3}{4} =$	12)	$\frac{12}{25} =$
5)	$\frac{3}{5} =$	13)	$\frac{1}{5} =$
6)	$\frac{8}{25} =$	14)	$\frac{3}{20} =$
7)	$\frac{4}{100} =$	15)	$\frac{35}{40} =$
8)	$\frac{75}{100} =$	16)	$\frac{3}{10} =$

To write more exercises, write down fractions for your child to change into decimals. To avoid answers with many numbers after the decimal point, only use fractions whose bottom numbers *cannot* be divided by three, seven, eleven, thirteen or seventeen.

Tackling the Exercise

If necessary, help your child to realize that he can answer the first question by using his basic knowledge of decimals. However, this technique won't work with the second question. If he doesn't know how to tackle it (or knows the answer from memory but doesn't know how to work it out), encourage him to think of the fraction as if it were a division question. Your conversation might sound like this:

YOU: Do you remember that we discovered that a fraction is another way of writing a division question?

CHILD: Yes.

YOU: So one half means the same as one divided by two, doesn't it?
(*Write* $\frac{1}{2} = 1 \div 2$.)

CHILD: But I can't work that out. It's too hard.

YOU: I know. That's why you're going to use this.

> (*Give him the calculator and, if necessary, show him how to use it.*)

Don't worry if he still uses the calculator when the questions involve tenths or hundredths. Just encourage him to look at his answer and realize he could've written it down straight away by using his knowledge of decimals.

Moving On

Stay on this level until your child can confidently change fractions into decimals using the calculator. Then move on to another topic.

24 / Percentages

Percentages are an excellent way of comparing similar quantities. Unfortunately the more unscrupulous members of society have found they're also an excellent way of confusing people. If you can give your child a good understanding of percentages, you won't just be helping her with her schoolwork. You'll be protecting her from being misled or cheated in the future.

What Are Percentages?

If someone offers you one sixth of a cake or three sixths of it, you can tell which is the largest piece without looking at them. However, if your choice is between five eighths and nine fifteenths, you won't know which is biggest unless you can actually see the pieces.

Because it's very hard to compare the size of fractions whose bottom numbers are different, mathematicians have agreed to use the same fractions most of the time. The ones they have chosen are hundredths and they call them percentages. Of course, lazy mathematicians want everything they write to be as simple as possible. That's why they write 54% instead of $\frac{54}{100}$.

Like all fractions, a percentage hasn't a fixed size. Half a large cake is bigger than half a small one and 10% of 10p is much less than 10% of £10. To judge the size of a percentage, we must know what it is a percentage of. Otherwise we can easily be misled.

Although percentages are usually taught as a separate subject, they're just hundredths written in a different way. Your child doesn't need to learn totally new skills to work with percentages. She just needs to learn how to apply the knowledge she already has about fractions and decimals.

INTRODUCING PERCENTAGES

Aim
To introduce percentages as an alternative way of writing hundredths.

Essential Background Knowledge
Before starting this work your child should know what fractions are and be able to write them.

Equipment
You'll need a knife and a bar of chocolate or something else your child likes to eat.

Tackling the Oral Work
Start the session with some counting or tables work. Then get out the chocolate and ask your child if she'd prefer to have six twenty-fourths or seven fourteenths. Talk about how difficult it is to compare fractions if the bottom numbers are different. Next ask your child if she'd like twenty-five hundredths or fifty hundredths of the chocolate. Give her whichever she chooses. (She may be surprised to realize it's a quarter or a half.)

While she's eating, talk about how much easier it was to compare the fractions when they were both hundredths. Explain that mathematicians have agreed to use hundredths most of the time when they need to talk about fractions, so that it's easier to tell which one is biggest. We call these fractions percentages and, instead of writing $\frac{25}{100}$ and $\frac{50}{100}$, we write 25% and 50% and say 25 per cent and 50 per cent.

Moving On

Once your child understands that percentages are just another way of writing hundredths, move on to another topic.

Useful Follow-up Work

Now help your child to notice how percentages are used in the world around her. When she sees one, encourage her to try to spot what it's a percentage of. This isn't always immediately obvious.

CHANGING PERCENTAGES INTO FRACTIONS AND DECIMALS

Essential Background Knowledge

Before starting this work your child should:

a) be able to change tenths and hundredths written as fractions into decimals

b) know that percentages are an alternative way of writing hundredths.

Before You Start the Session

Write these questions in your child's book:

1) $34\% = \frac{}{100} = 0\cdot$	6) $60\% = \frac{}{100} = 0\cdot$
2) $46\% = \frac{}{100} = 0\cdot$	7) $99\% = \frac{}{100} = 0\cdot$
3) $70\% = \frac{}{100} = 0\cdot$	8) $30\% = \frac{}{100} = 0\cdot$
4) $5\% = \frac{}{100} = 0\cdot$	9) $6\% = \frac{}{100} = 0\cdot$
5) $3\% = \frac{}{100} = 0\cdot$	10) $25\% = \frac{}{100} = 0\cdot$

To write more exercises, make up similar questions which ask your child to turn percentages into fractions and decimals.

Tackling the Exercise

Before your child starts work, explain that you want her to fill in the gaps in each question. Be willing to work with her until she is confident enough to work alone. Her answers should look like this:

1) $34\% = \frac{34}{100} = 0.34$
3) $70\% = \frac{70}{100} = 0.7$

You may need to remind her that, when she turns 60% into a decimal, she can write 0·6 rather than 0·60.

Watch her carefully when she reaches question 4. This is a little more tricky because there are no tenths. If she writes 0·5, point out her mistake as gently as possible. Then help her to realize that the five will only mean five hundredths if she puts it in the hundredths position, so she needs to put a zero in the tenths position (0·05). If she has trouble understanding this, encourage her to think how she would write one pound and five pence.

Moving On
Stay at this level until your child can confidently change percentages to both fractions and decimals. Then move on to changing decimals into percentages or another topic.

CHANGING DECIMALS INTO PERCENTAGES

Essential Background Knowledge
Before starting this work your child should:

a) be able to change decimals to fractions (revise this before you start this section if your child hasn't practised it recently.
b) understand that percentages are a different way of writing hundredths
c) be able to multiply a decimal by a hundred.

Before You Start the Session
Write the exercise on the next page in your child's book:

1) $0.75 = \frac{}{100} = $ %   7) $0.3 = \frac{}{100} = $ %
2) $0.32 = \frac{}{100} = $ %   8) $0.6 = \frac{}{100} = $ %
3) $0.25 = \frac{}{100} = $ %   9) $0.47 = \frac{}{100} = $ %
4) $0.03 = \frac{}{100} = $ %   10) $0.7 = \frac{}{100} = $ %
5) $0.12 = \frac{}{100} = $ %   11) $0.05 = \frac{}{100} = $ %
6) $0.07 = \frac{}{100} = $ %   12) $0.92 = \frac{}{100} = $ %

To write more exercises, make up similar questions which ask your child to change a decimal into a percentage. Only use numbers which are less than one and which have no more than two numbers after the decimal point. Once your child understands what to do, you needn't write in the middle step involving changing the decimal into a fraction.

Tackling the Exercise

Before your child starts work, make sure she understands that you want her to fill in the gaps in the questions. Be prepared to work with her, if necessary, until she understands what to do. Her answers should look like this:

$$1) \quad 0.75 = \frac{75}{100} = 75\%$$

If she seems uncertain when she reaches question 4, remind her that the three means three hundredths (the zero in the tenths position is there to make sure the three is in the right place). Once she realizes this, the question is no harder than those she has already done.

Watch her carefully when she tackles question 7 as the lack of a number in the hundredths position may fool her into making a mistake. Her answer should look like this:

$$7) \quad 0.3 = \frac{30}{100} = 30\%$$

If she writes three in the top of the fraction, suggest she thinks again. If she doesn't spot her mistake straight away, ask her what the three is telling her about. Is it tenths or hundredths? When she's realized that she has three tenths, ask her how many hundredths that is. If she's not sure, encourage her to imagine the question is about money and ask her how many pennies are the same as three 10ps.

When she's successfully completed the exercise, encourage her to look at the questions and answers again to see if she can spot how to find the percentage directly without changing the decimal into a fraction first. If necessary, help her to see that she could just multiply the decimal by a hundred.

Moving On
Stay on this level until your child can confidently change a decimal to a percentage. Then move on to another topic.

CHANGING FRACTIONS INTO PERCENTAGES

Essential Background Knowledge
Before starting this work your child should:
a) know that a fraction is another way of writing division
b) be able to change a fraction to a decimal by dividing the top number by the bottom one
c) be able to change a decimal to a percentage.

Before You Start
Before you start this topic, include some revision questions in your child's written work which ask her to turn fractions into decimals. When you're sure this work is fresh in her mind, write this exercise in her book:

1) $\frac{1}{10} = 0 \cdot \quad = \quad \%$ 7) $\frac{4}{5} = 0 \cdot \quad = \quad \%$

2) $\frac{1}{2} = 0 \cdot \quad = \quad \%$ 8) $\frac{14}{50} = 0 \cdot \quad = \quad \%$

3) $\frac{76}{100} = 0 \cdot \quad = \quad \%$ 9) $\frac{3}{4} = 0 \cdot \quad = \quad \%$

4) $\frac{1}{4} = 0 \cdot \quad = \quad \%$ 10) $\frac{9}{20} = 0 \cdot \quad = \quad \%$

5) $\frac{5}{10} = 0 \cdot \quad = \quad \%$ 11) $\frac{5}{8} = 0 \cdot \quad = \quad \%$

6) $\frac{56}{100} = 0 \cdot \quad = \quad \%$ 12) $\frac{2}{5} = 0 \cdot \quad = \quad \%$

To write more exercises, write down fractions for your child to turn into percentages. Choose fractions which will change to decimals with no more than three numbers after the decimal point. Check this with a calculator before you give the questions to your child. You'll find it easiest if you avoid fractions whose bottom number can be divided by three, seven or eleven. Those with two, four, five, eight, ten, twenty, twenty-five, fifty or one hundred as their bottom number are all safe choices.

Tackling the Exercise

Changing fractions into percentages is really a two-stage process although sometimes the two stages are written down as if they're one.

The first step is to change the fraction into a decimal. That's easy if the fraction is in tenths or hundredths. For other fractions, your child can use the calculator to divide the top number by the bottom one. (Don't worry if she uses it for tenths and hundredths as well: just point out that it's not really necessary.)

The second stage is to change the decimal into a percentage by multiplying it by a hundred.

Your child already has the two skills she needs for this topic. She just needs to realize what she has to do and then practise until she can tackle the questions easily. Be prepared to work through the questions with her until she gains enough confidence to work alone.

BY THE WAY

Your child's teacher may tell her to change fractions into percentages by multiplying by a hundred. This is actually the same process as we've used but with the two steps combined into one.

Moving On

Stay on this level until your child can answer the questions confidently and accurately. Then move on to another topic.

FINDING A PERCENTAGE OF A NUMBER

Essential Background Knowledge
Before starting this topic your child should:
a) understand what percentages are
b) be able to multiply and divide by small numbers
c) be able to divide by a hundred.

Before You Start the Session
Write this exercise in your child's book, leaving at least three lines between the questions:

1)	10% of 200 =	6)	70% of 625 =
2)	30% of 400 =	7)	13% of 125 =
3)	20% of 300 =	8)	20% of 90 =
4)	15% of 200 =	9)	10% of 210 =
5)	32% of 50 =	10)	50% of 400 =

To write more exercises, make up similar questions asking your child to find a percentage of any number.

Tackling the Exercise
If your child already knows (and can remember) how to find a fraction of a number, she may use that skill to find the answer. Her answer will look like this:

$$10\% \text{ of } 200 = \tfrac{10}{100} \times 200 = 10 \times 2 = 20$$

If she doesn't use this method by herself, work with her to help her see how to tackle the question. Your conversation might sound like this:

YOU: What's the question asking you to do?
CHILD: I've got to find 10% of 200?
YOU: That sounds tricky. Let's think of something easier first. What's 1% of 200?
CHILD: I don't know.

> YOU: Can you remember what fraction means the same as 1%?
>
> CHILD: One hundredth.
>
> YOU: That's right. So 1% of 200 is exactly the same as one hundredth of 200 which is . . .?
>
> CHILD: Two.
>
> YOU: Good. Let's write that down before we forget.
> (*Under the questions write 1% of 200 is 2.*)
> Now if 1% of 200 is 2, what's 2% of 200?
>
> CHILD: Four.
>
> YOU: And 3% of 200?
>
> CHILD: Six.
>
> YOU: And 10% of 200?
>
> CHILD: Twenty.
>
> YOU: Well done. That's the answer you wanted. Let's write it in.
> (*Under your last comment write*
> *10% of 200 is 10 × 2 = 20.*)
> Now let's try the next one.

Keep working with your child until she feels confident enough to gradually start working on her own. Let her use the calculator when she meets numbers which she can't work out easily in her head.

For each question, encourage her to write down the stages of her working in the same way as you did. It'll help her to remember what she's doing and build good habits for more advanced work in years to come.

REMEMBER
To find any percentage of a number, start by finding 1%.

Moving On
Stay on this topic until your child can find any percentage of a

number confidently and accurately, using a calculator where necessary. Then move on to another topic.

WRITING ONE NUMBER AS A PERCENTAGE OF ANOTHER

Essential Background Knowledge
Before starting this work your child should:
a) know that percentages are a different way of writing hundredths
b) be able to change a fraction into a percentage by changing it into a decimal and multiplying by a hundred
c) be able to write one number as a fraction of another.

Before You Start
Write this exercise in your child's book, leaving at least three lines between the questions:

1)   Write 3 as a percentage of 4
2)   Write 15 as a percentage of 25
3)   Write 8 as a percentage of 32
4)   Write 20 as a percentage of 40
5)   Write 27 as a percentage of 50
6)   Write 6 as a percentage of 24
7)   Write 14 as a percentage of 35
8)   Write 3 as a percentage of 30
9)   Write 7 as a percentage of 56
10)   Write 24 as a percentage of 30

To write more exercises, make up similar questions asking your child to write one number as a percentage of another larger one.

Tackling the Exercise
These questions may look frightening to your child, especially if she's been taught this topic unsuccessfully in the past. Be prepared to reassure her that she's mastered all the skills she

needs to answer them successfully. If she's not sure how to tackle the first question, look at it together. Your conversation might sound like this:

YOU: Let's go back to something I know you can do very well. What's three written as a fraction of four?

CHILD: Three quarters.

YOU: Good. We'll write that down before we forget. (*Write $\frac{3}{4}$ under the question.*)
Now, can you remember how to turn that fraction into a decimal?

CHILD: You divide the three by the four.

YOU: That's right. Use the calculator to work it out.

CHILD: It's 0·75.

YOU: That's right.
(*Write $= 0\cdot75$ after the previous answer.*)
Now, how can we turn that decimal into a percentage?

CHILD: Times it by a hundred.

YOU: And the answer's . . .?

CHILD: Seventy-five.

YOU: Well done. So three is 75% of four.
(*Write $= 75\%$ after your previous answer.*)
You see, you already know enough to do these questions. Let's try the next one.

IMPORTANT

The answer to this question should look like this:
$\frac{3}{4} = 0\cdot75 = 75\%$
Don't write
$\frac{3}{4} = 0\cdot75 = 0\cdot75 \times 100 = 75\%$
because 0·75 and 0·75 × 100 are not equal.

Keep working with your child for as long as necessary. With each question, stress the same sequence of work:

a) write the first number as a fraction of the second
b) change the fraction to a decimal
c) change the decimal to a percentage.

Moving On
Stay on this level until your child can answer the questions confidently and accurately. Then move on to another topic.

Further Work
When your child's schoolwork involves percentage questions written in words, she may find it difficult to decide which skills she needs to use. Encourage her to read each question carefully before she decides how to tackle it. If a percentage is given, help her to spot which number it's a percentage of. If she's asked to calculate a percentage, help her to spot which two numbers are involved and which one's going to be the percentage of the other.

25 / Multiplying by Large Numbers

In real life, most people use a calculator to multiply two numbers which are both larger than ten. However, there's not always one available at the crucial moment, so we need to know how to work out the answer by ourselves. That's why long multiplication is still taught in schools.

Be careful not to rush into this chapter too soon. Wait until your child can confidently multiply large numbers by numbers no larger than ten. Otherwise he may end up thoroughly confused.

But my child has just started long multiplication at school. I've got to help him with it now.

If he still finds ordinary multiplication very difficult, long multiplication will probably seem completely incomprehensible. Help him to see that he's finding the work hard because he hasn't got the necessary background. Reassure him that he's not stupid but just has some gaps in his knowledge. If he agrees, you could write to his teacher to explain the situation.

If he does understand how to do ordinary multiplication but doesn't know all his tables, work through the steps in this chapter using only the tables which he does know. Once he understands the method, he can use his table square to help him tackle the harder questions he meets at school.

Before You Start

Before you start this work, spend at least a couple of sessions practising tables and written multiplication questions so these skills are fresh in your child's mind.

Step 1

Aims
To introduce the quick way to multiply by ten.

Essential Background Knowledge
Before starting this work your child should:
a) be able to multiply by numbers less than ten.
b) know his ten times table.

Before You Start the Session
Write this exercise in your child's book:

1)	25 × 10	5)	267 × 10

2)	56 × 10	6)	435 × 10

3)	62 × 10	7)	258 × 10

4)	83 × 10	8)	1354 × 10

$$9) \qquad 8765 \qquad 10) \qquad 75$$
$$\times \underline{10} \qquad \qquad \times \underline{10}$$

To write more exercises, make up questions involving multiplying numbers greater than ten by ten.

Tackling the Exercise

Because your child knows his ten times table, he can answer these questions in exactly the same way as he would multiply by smaller numbers. Once he realizes this, he should be able to work out the answers without much trouble.

When he's successfully finished the exercise, ask him if he can see any connection between the questions and the answers. He may find this easier if you write them side by side in a list like this:

$$25 \qquad 250$$
$$56 \qquad 560$$
$$62 \qquad 620$$

(and so on).

When he's spotted that the answers look the same as the questions but have a zero at the end, talk about what's really happened. Help him to see that all the figures in the question have moved one place to the left: the ones have become tens, the tens have become hundreds and the hundreds have become thousands. That leaves nothing in the ones position, so we put a zero there.

In future exercises, encourage your child to practise multiplying by ten quickly by moving all the figures one place to the left.

But isn't it easier to say that to multiply by ten, you add a zero?

It may be easier but it isn't true because this simplified rule only works for whole numbers, not decimals (10×1.75 is 17.5 not 1.750). It's much better to help him understand what's really happening rather than teach him something he'll need to unlearn later.

Moving On

Stay on this level until your child can confidently use this method to multiply by ten without help from you. Then move on to step 2 in your next session.

Step 2

Aim

To introduce multiplying by a hundred.

Essential Background

Before starting this work your child should:

a) be able to multiply by any number less than ten

b) know the quick way to multiply by ten

c) be able to count in hundreds.

Before You Start the Session

Write this exercise in your child's book:

1)	$2 \times 100 =$	7)	$\begin{array}{r} 72 \\ \times\ 100 \\ \hline \end{array}$
2)	$5 \times 100 =$		
3)	$9 \times 100 =$		
4)	$7 \times 100 =$	8)	$\begin{array}{r} 165 \\ \times\ 100 \\ \hline \end{array}$
5)	$\begin{array}{r} 24 \\ \times\ 100 \\ \hline \end{array}$	9)	$\begin{array}{r} 521 \\ \times\ 100 \\ \hline \end{array}$
6)	$\begin{array}{r} 39 \\ \times\ 100 \\ \hline \end{array}$	10)	$\begin{array}{r} 31 \\ \times\ 100 \\ \hline \end{array}$

To write more exercises, make up similar questions involving multiplying by a hundred.

Tackling the Exercise
If your child isn't sure how to tackle the first four questions, encourage him to count in hundreds to find the answers.

When he reaches question 5, point out that he can tackle it in the same way as he does when he multiplies by a smaller number. When he's multiplied the four by a hundred, he may not be sure what to do with the 400. Help him to realize that he has no ones, so he can put a zero in the ones position. He also has no tens to carry to the tens column (he can put a zero under the line if he likes), but he does have four hundreds to carry to the hundreds column so he should write a four in the correct place under the line like this:

$$\begin{array}{r} 24 \\ \times\ 100 \\ \hline 0 \\ \hline 40 \end{array}$$

He can then multiply the two tens by a hundred to find he has 200 tens. That means he has no tens, so he can put a zero in the tens column, no hundreds to carry to the hundreds column (he can out a zero under the line if he likes) and two thousands to carry to the thousands column like this:

$$\begin{array}{r} 24 \\ \times\ 100 \\ \hline 00 \\ \hline 40 \\ 20 \end{array}$$

Finally he can write the two thousands and the four hundreds he has carried into the answer like this:

$$\begin{array}{r} 24 \\ \times 100 \\ \hline 2400 \\ \end{array}$$
40
20

Keep helping him like this for the rest of the exercise if necessary but, if he looks really confused, let him use a calculator to find the answer. He won't be working out similar questions this way in the future, so it doesn't matter if he doesn't gain enough confidence to work alone.

When he's finished the work, encourage him to look carefully at his answers. Help him to see that each figure in the question has moved two places to the left which leaves zeros in the tens position and the ones position. You can compare this with what happens when you multiply by ten. In future exercises, let him practise multiplying by a hundred quickly by moving each figure in the number two places to the left.

Moving On
Stay on this level until your child can confidently use the quick method to multiply by a hundred without any help from you. Then move on to step 3 or another topic.

Step 3

Aim
To introduce multiplying by twenty, thirty, forty, etcetera.

Essential Background Knowledge
Before starting this work your child should:
a) be able to multiply by numbers less than ten
b) be able to multiply by ten using the quick method

c) understand that multiplying is the same as adding over and over again.

Before You Start the Session
Write this exercise in your child's book leaving at least two lines between each question:

1)	$14 \times 20 =$	7)	$21 \times 50 =$
2)	$13 \times 30 =$	8)	$45 \times 20 =$
3)	$15 \times 20 =$	9)	$39 \times 50 =$
4)	$21 \times 30 =$	10)	$243 \times 50 =$
5)	$23 \times 20 =$	11)	$192 \times 20 =$
6)	$14 \times 50 =$	12)	$23 \times 20 =$

To write more exercises, make up questions involving multiplying any number between eleven and a thousand by twenty, thirty, forty, fifty, sixty, seventy, eighty or ninety. Concentrate on the tables your child knows best until he understands what he has to do.

Tackling the Exercise
If your child looks worried or doesn't know how to start, work with him to explain how to tackle these questions. Your conversation might sound like this:

YOU: Do you remember that multiplying is the same as adding over and over again? That's how you work out the answers to your tables when you get stuck, isn't it?

CHILD: Yes.

YOU: So 14×20 means twenty fourteens added together. That would be a very long sum if you wrote all those fourteens down one after the other.

CHILD: I'd keep losing my place.

YOU: So would I. It'd be a lot easier if we wrote the fourteens down like this.

(Write the following on some spare paper.)

14	14
14	14
14	14
14	14
14	14
14	14
14	14
14	14
14	14
14	14

How many fourteens are there in each column?

CHILD: Ten.

YOU: So what does the first column add up to?

(Child starts to add up the numbers.)

That looks like hard work. Don't forget that adding ten fourteens is the same as multiplying fourteen by ten.

CHILD: Oh, it's 140!

YOU: Good. What about the other column?

CHILD: That's 140 too.

YOU: That's right, so now we just need to add the two 140s together to get the answer. Or, if you prefer, you can multiply 140 by two: remember that's the same thing really. *(He can work this out on some spare paper if he wants to.)*

CHILD: It's 280.

YOU: Well done. So you've multiplied by twenty by multiplying by ten first and then by two. Let's write that down.

(Write down the answer showing the working like this:

1) $14 \times 20 = 14 \times 10 \times 2$
                $= 140 \times 2 = 280$)

Now let's try the next one.

Keep helping your child like this until he gains enough confidence to start working by himself. Don't worry if you need to write out the addition in full for several questions before he gets the idea. It's worth spending time now to make sure he really understands what he's doing.

When I multiply by twenty I never write down that middle step about multiplying by ten. Why do I have to do that when I'm helping my child?

It'll help him remember what he's doing. As he gains confidence and competence, he may start to do the whole question in his head as you do but don't rush him into doing this if he doesn't want to. Let him continue to write that middle step for as long as he feels he needs it.

Moving On
Stay on this level until your child can answer the questions easily and confidently. Then move on to step 4, step 5 or another topic.

Step 4

Aim
To introduce multiplying by 200, 300, etcetera.

Essential Background Knowledge
Before starting this work your child should:
a) be able to multiply by numbers less than ten
b) be able to multiply by a hundred using the quick method
c) understand that multiplying is the same as adding over and over again.
d) be able to multiply by twenty, thirty, forty . . .

Before You Start the Session
Write this exercise in your child's book, leaving at least one line between each question:

1) $13 \times 200 =$	7) $211 \times 800 =$
2) $15 \times 300 =$	8) $143 \times 500 =$
3) $14 \times 500 =$	9) $72 \times 300 =$
4) $21 \times 200 =$	10) $542 \times 200 =$
5) $45 \times 500 =$	11) $222 \times 500 =$
6) $67 \times 300 =$	12) $111 \times 900 =$

To write extra exercises, if necessary, make up questions involving multiplying any number between eleven and a thousand by 200, 300, 400, 500, 600, 700, 800 or 900. Concentrate on the tables your child knows best until he understands what to do.

Tackling the Exercise
The method for multiplying by 200, 300 and so on is just an extension of the one introduced in the previous step. First of all you multiply by a hundred and then by the number of hundreds. So the answers to the exercise should look like this:

1) $13 \times 200 = 1300 \times 2 = 2600$
2) $15 \times 300 = 1500 \times 3 = 4500$
(etcetera)

Your child may realize this straight away. If not, talk him through the questions in the same way as you did in step 3. But don't try to write out thirteen two hundred times though: you risk writer's cramp and terminal boredom. Let your child use his imagination and the knowledge he has already gained about multiplying by twenty and thirty.

Moving On
Stay on this level until your child can answer the questions confidently and accurately. Then move on to step 5 or another topic.

Step 5

Aim:
To introduce long multiplication.

Essential Background Knowledge
Before starting this work your child should:
a) be able to multiply large numbers by numbers less than ten
b) be able to multiply by twenty, thirty, forty . . .
c) know that multiplying is the same as adding over and over
   again.

Equipment
You will need some pieces of paper or card (four 8 cm × 6 cm
and five 4 cm × 6 cm) similar to the ones you used in chapter
13 to teach place value. Mark the large ones with ten, twenty,
thirty and fifty respectively and the small ones with one, two,
four, five and six.

Before You Start the Session
Write the following exercise in your child's book. Leave a
large space to the left of each question and at least four lines
under each one.

1)   21   4)   281
         × 14   × 15

2)   76   5)   95
         × 21   × 52

3)   121   6)   123
         × 36   × 25

To write more exercises, make up questions asking your child to multiply a number between eleven and a thousand by another number between eleven and ninety-nine. At first, concentrate on the tables your child knows best until he understands the method.

Tackling the Exercise
If your child doesn't know what to do, work through the first question with him in stages:

Stage 1
Point out that he could easily work out 21 × 2 or 21 × 8. The only reason this question is difficult is that he doesn't know his fourteen times table. That's not his fault. No one expects him to know it.

Stage 2
Remind him that 21 × 14 means fourteen twenty-ones added together. Write them down on a spare piece of paper with ten of the twenty-ones in one column and the remaining four in another like this:

21	21
21	21
21	21
21	21
21	
21	
21	
21	
21	
21	

Point out that adding all those fourteens one after the other would be quite tricky; he'd probably keep losing his place. It would be much easier to add the column of ten and the column of four and then add the two answers together.

Help your child to see that that is the same as working out 21 × 10 and 21 × 4 and adding the two answers together.

Stage 3

Now you've explained the principle behind long multiplication, you need to help your child put the process down on paper. Look at the question in his book again and remind him that you're multiplying by fourteen. Place the 4 card on top of the 10 card so it covers the zero and only 14 is visible like this:

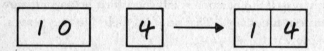

Suggest that he starts by multiplying by the 4. Write what he's doing by the side of the question like this:

$$
\begin{array}{r}
21 \\
\times\ \underline{14} \\
\end{array}
$$

21 × 4 =

Let him work out the multiplication himself (with help, if necessary) and write the answer down under the question with the numbers in the correct columns like this:

$$
\begin{array}{r}
21 \\
\times\ \underline{14} \\
84 \\
\end{array}
$$

21 × 4 =

He's finished with the 4 now so take that card away to reveal the 10 underneath which will remind him that the next step is to multiply by the 10. Write that in like this:

```
                              21
                         ×    14
         21 × 4 =             84
         21 × 10 =
```

Let your child work out the answer and write it in the correct place:

```
                              21
                         ×    14
         21 × 4 =             84
         21 × 10 =           210
```

Now let him add his two intermediate answers together to find the final one:

```
                              21
                         ×    14
         21 × 4 =             84
         21 × 10 =           210
                            ─────
                             294
```

Your child has now successfully answered the first question. This is a big achievement so make sure you tell him how pleased you are before he moves on to the next one.

Tackle the rest of the exercise in the same way but only use the number cards as a visual reminder if your child finds them helpful. When the number contains more than one ten, write the question like this:

```
2)                                        76
                                     ×    21
                  76 × 1 =                76
         76 × 20 = 760 × 2 =            1520
                                       ─────
                                        1596
```

I wasn't taught to write things like 76 × 1 and 76 × 20 by the side of a long multiplication question. Are they really necessary?

They're not essential but they'll help your child understand and remember what he's doing. He can stop writing these instructions down as soon as he feels they're no longer necessary but don't rush him into giving them up before he feels ready. If he wants to put them in his school work but his teacher objects, suggest that he writes them in pencil and erases them once he's finished the question.

You suggest my child should multiply by the ones first and then by the tens but his teacher has told him to start with the tens and then multiply by the ones.

As long as you multiply by the tens figure and the ones figure, it doesn't matter which you do first. Your child will probably be happier working in the same order he's been taught at school.

Moving On
Stay on this level until your child can answer the questions confidently and accurately. Then move on to step 6 or another topic.

Step 6

Aim
To extend long multiplication to larger numbers.

Essential Background Knowledge
Before starting this work your child should:
a) be able to multiply by any number less than a hundred
b) be able to multiply by 200, 300, 400 . . .

Before You Start the Session
Write this exercise in your child's book. Make sure you leave plenty of room for the working:

1)	345	3)		836
	× 211		×	205

2)	531	4)		523
	× 125		×	121

To write more exercises, make up questions involving multiplying two numbers which are both between 100 and 999.

Tackling the Exercise
The method used for these questions is exactly the same as that used in step 4 except that your child will need to multiply by the hundreds figure as well as by the tens and the units. You can adapt the ideas in step 4 to explain this. His answer to the first question should look like this:

1)
$$
\begin{array}{r}
345 \\
\times\ \underline{211} \\
345 \times 1 = \quad 345 \\
345 \times 10 = \quad 3450 \\
345 \times 200 = 34500 \times 2 = \quad \underline{69000} \\
\underline{72795}
\end{array}
$$

Moving On
Stay on this level until your child can answer the questions confidently with only occasional mistakes. Then move on to another topic.

REVISION IS IMPORTANT

Remember to include occasional long multiplication questions in your revision work. Otherwise your child may forget how to tackle them.

Does the mention of long division send shivers down your spine? Does it bring back memories of questions which look like this?

$$
\begin{array}{r}
2\ 5\ 1 \\
17\overline{)4\,2\,6\,7} \\
\underline{3\,4} \\
8\,6 \\
\underline{8\,5} \\
1\,7
\end{array}
$$

Then I've got good news for you. Contrary to popular belief, dividing by large numbers is exactly the same process as dividing by small ones. Long division isn't a separate process. It only looks different because it's become traditional to show some of the working.

This is supposed to make long division easier but it often doesn't have that effect at all. If you don't understand what's happening, those numbers under the question easily appear to have magic powers beyond the comprehension of all except the most mathematically gifted.

I'm going to make a revolutionary suggestion. If showing the working doesn't help, *don't do it*. There's no reason why you can't write down long division in exactly the same way as you write other division questions. For instance, the earlier example would look like this:

$$
\begin{array}{r}
2\ 5\ 1 \\
17\overline{)4\,2^{8}6^{1}7}
\end{array}
$$

*My child is confused by the traditional method of setting
down long division but her teacher tells her off if she doesn't
use it.*

There are two ways you can handle this. Firstly you can go to
her school and ask the teacher why he's being inflexible. (On
no account do this without your child's agreement.) If he
replies that he needs to see the working to follow what your
child's doing, point out that the working is still there. It's just
on the side of the page instead of under the sum.

If this doesn't have the desired effect or if your child doesn't
want you to go to her school, work through this chapter until
she understands the method. Then you can show her how to
set down the working to please her teacher.

*Now everyone uses calculators, does my child really need to
learn long division at all?*

She's very unlikely to need to use it in real life so only work
through this chapter if you're sure she needs to be able to do
long division at school.

Step 1

Aim
To revise division by whole numbers less than ten so that the
process is fresh in your child's mind.

Essential Background Knowledge
Before starting this work your child should:
a) know her tables well
b) be able to divide by any whole number less than 10.

Before You Start the Session

Write this exercise in your child's book:

1) $3\overline{)\ 639}$	6) $7\overline{)\ 861}$
2) $4\overline{)\ 944}$	7) $8\overline{)\ 256}$
3) $5\overline{)\ 340}$	8) $5\overline{)\ 570}$
4) $2\overline{)\ 478}$	9) $3\overline{)\ 195}$
5) $3\overline{)\ 546}$	10) $2\overline{)\ 716}$

To write more exercises, make up questions involving dividing numbers greater than a hundred by whole numbers less than ten. Make all the numbers divide exactly without any remainders.

Tackling the Exercise

Don't worry if your child's a little hesitant at first because she hasn't done any similar questions for a while. If necessary, work with her until she regains her confidence. Encourage her to talk about what she's doing as she works, so you can make sure she really understands the method she's using. For instance, with question 2, her thinking should sound something like this:

How many fours in nine?

Two and one left over.

Write down the two and change the one hundred left over into ten tens, so we've got fourteen tens.

$$4\overline{)9\ '4\ 4}^{\ 2}$$

How many fours in fourteen?
Three and two left over.
Write down the three and change the two tens left over into twenty ones so we've got twenty-four ones.

$$\begin{array}{r} 2\ 3 \\ 4\overline{)9\,{}^1 4\,{}^2 4} \end{array}$$

How many fours in twenty-four?
Six.
Write down the six and the answer is 236.

$$\begin{array}{r} 2\ 3\ 6 \\ 4\overline{)9\,{}^1 4\,{}^2 4} \end{array}$$

Moving On
Stay on this level until your child can answer the questions accurately and confidently with only occasional help. Then move on to step 2.

Step 2

Aim
To introduce dividing by numbers greater than ten.

Essential Background Knowledge
Before starting this work your child should:
a) know her tables well
b) be able to divide by any whole number less than ten
c) be able to multiply large numbers by any whole number less than ten.

Before You Start the Session

Write this exercise in your child's book. Put the questions down the left-hand side of the page leaving the right-hand side for her working:

1)
$$5\overline{)60}$$

2)
$$13\overline{)39}$$

3)
$$21\overline{)63}$$

4)
$$25\overline{)125}$$

5)
$$17\overline{)68}$$

6)
$$41\overline{)82}$$

7)
$$16\overline{)96}$$

8)
$$5\overline{)45}$$

To write more exercises, make up questions asking your child to divide by numbers greater than ten. Make sure all the questions divide exactly without any remainders and that the answers are nine or less. The easiest way to do this is to choose the answer you want and multiply it by the number by which you're dividing to find the question. For instance, for question 2, I multiplied thirteen by three to find thirty-nine. (Use a calculator. It saves a lot of hard work.)

Tackling the Exercise

This is the first time you've asked your child to divide by a number greater than ten, so she'll probably feel worried and won't know what to do. Reassure her that you're confident she'll be able to manage and work with her until she understands what she's doing. Your conversation about question 2 might sound like this:

YOU: It's not really as hard as it looks.

CHILD: But I don't know my thirteen times table.

YOU: I know you don't. Neither do I.

CHILD: So how am I supposed to do the question?

YOU: We've just got to guess and then see if we're right. If we're not, we can have another try.

CHILD: Eh?

YOU: Well, thirteen is just a bit bigger than ten and thirty-nine is almost forty. Now how many tens are there in forty?

CHILD: Four.

YOU: So let's start our guessing there. We need to find out what four thirteens are.
(Write 13 × 4 =   on the right-hand side of the page and let your child work out the answer.)

CHILD: It's fifty-two. That's too big.

YOU: Never mind. Let's try again. Four is too big so we'll try three.
(Write 13 × 3 =   on the right-hand side of the page and let your child work out the answer.)

CHILD: It's thirty-nine. So thirty-nine divided by thirteen is three.

YOU: Good. I knew you could do it. Write in the answer then and we'll try the next one.

BY THE WAY

It's a good idea to make sure your first guess is wrong. Then your child won't feel so bad if she doesn't guess the right answer first time herself.

Keep helping in this way until your child has gained enough confidence to start working by herself. If necessary, reassure her occasionally that it isn't cheating to work out the multiplications on the side of the page and that it doesn't matter if she takes a long time to find the answer.

Moving On
Stay on this level until your child can answer the questions confidently and competently. Don't worry if this takes some time. It's important not to rush this stage. Then move on to step 3.

Step 3

Aim
To practise dividing by large numbers where the answer includes a remainder.

Essential Background Knowledge
Don't start this work until your child has successfully completed the previous step.

Before You Start the Session
Write this exercise in your child's book. Put the questions down the left-hand side of the page with at least three lines between each one:

1)
$$21 \overline{)\ 84}$$

2)
$$14 \overline{)\ 58}$$

3)
$$15 \overline{)\ 100}$$

4)
$$23 \overline{)\ 107}$$

5)
$$17 \overline{)\ 46}$$

6)
$$31 \overline{)\ 62}$$

To write more exercises, make up questions involving dividing by numbers greater than ten where some of the answers include a remainder. In each question, make the larger number less than ten times the size of the smaller one.

Tackling the Exercise

Before your child starts the exercise, point out that when the questions don't divide exactly, you want her to write the answers with a remainder. (Otherwise she may give the answer as a decimal instead if she's already learnt how to do this.)

Watch her carefully as she tackles the second question, so you can offer help as soon as she needs it. Once she has found that 14 × 4 is 56, she may realize straight away that the answer is four. Don't worry if she needs to check for herself that 14 × 5 is too big.

Because the remainder here is small, she may work it out in her head. If not, suggest that she works out the subtraction on the side of the page in the same way as she has for the multiplication. When she's finished the question successfully, explain that sometimes people work out the subtraction under the question. Instead of writing:

$$14\overline{)58} \quad \overset{4\ \text{rem}\,2}{} \qquad \times \overset{1\,4}{\underset{56}{4}} \qquad -\overset{58}{\underset{2}{\underline{56}}}$$

they write:

$$14\overline{)\begin{array}{l}\overset{4\ \text{rem}\,2}{58}\\ \underline{56}\\ \ \ 2\end{array}} \qquad \times\overset{1\,4}{\underset{\underline{56}}{4}}$$

The two methods are just different ways of writing down the same thing. Let your child use whichever one she prefers.

Moving On
Once your child can work out the remainders confidently and accurately, move on to step 4.

Step 4

Aim
To extend your child's skills to questions whose answers are greater than ten.

Essential Background Knowledge
Don't start this work until your child has successfully completed the previous two steps.

Before You Start the Session
Write this exercise in your child's book. Put the questions down the left-hand side of the page leaving at least four lines between each question:

$$1) \quad 25\overline{)\ 125}$$

$$2) \quad 25\overline{)\ 525}$$

$$3) \quad 17\overline{)\ 357}$$

$$4) \quad 21\overline{)\ 735}$$

$$5) \quad 21\overline{)\ 126}$$

To write more exercises, make up similar questions involving dividing numbers between a hundred and a thousand by numbers between ten and ninety-nine. Use a calculator to help you

choose the numbers so the answers are greater than ten and
have no remainders.

Tackling the Exercise
When your child reaches question 2, she'll find she cannot just
guess the answer because it's bigger than ten. Be prepared to
work with her and encourage her to tackle the question in the
following stages:
a) Look first at the two in the hundreds position. How many
   fourteens are there in two?
   None, so change the two hundreds into twenty tens, which
   means you now have twenty-nine tens.

$$14\overline{)2\,^29\,4}$$

b) How many fourteens are there in twenty-nine?
   Experiment to find that $14 \times 2 = 28$ and $29 - 28 = 1$
   Write down the two in the tens position of the answer.
   Then change the one ten left over into ten ones, so you
   now have fourteen ones altogether.

$$14\overline{)2\,^29\,^14} \qquad \begin{array}{r} 14 \\ \times\ 2 \\ \hline 28 \end{array} \qquad \begin{array}{r} 29 \\ -28 \\ \hline 1 \end{array}$$

or

$$14\overline{)2\,^29\,^14} \\ \underline{\ 2\ 8} \\ 1 \qquad \begin{array}{r} 14 \\ \times\ 2 \\ \hline 28 \end{array}$$

Only use the second method if your child found it useful
in the previous step.

c) How many fourteens in fourteen?

One. Write that down and the completed question will
look like this:

$$
14 \overline{\smash)2\,^2 9\,^1 4} \qquad \begin{array}{r} 14 \\ \times\ 2 \\ \hline 28 \end{array} \qquad \begin{array}{r} 29 \\ -\ 28 \\ \hline 1 \end{array}
$$

with quotient $2\,1$

or this:

$$
\begin{array}{r} 2\,1 \\ 14 \overline{\smash)2\,^2 9\,^1 4} \\ 2\,8 \\ \hline 1 \end{array} \qquad \begin{array}{r} 14 \\ \times\ 2 \\ \hline 28 \end{array}
$$

Continue to work with your child until she understands
what to do and is confident enough to work alone.

Moving On

Stay on this level until your child can answer the questions
confidently and accurately, setting the questions down in whichever way she prefers. Then move on to step 5 or on to another
topic.

Step 5

Aim

To extend the techniques learnt so far to dividing numbers
greater than a thousand.

Essential Background Knowledge
Don't start this work until your child has successfully completed
the previous step.

Before You Start the Session
Write this exercise in your child's book. Put the questions
down the left-hand side of the page leaving at least five lines
between each question.

1)
$$13\overline{)\ 403}$$

2)
$$17\overline{)\ 2431}$$

3)
$$23\overline{)\ 5635}$$

4)
$$21\overline{)\ 6741}$$

To write more exercises, make up questions involving dividing a
number greater than a thousand by a number greater than ten.
Choose the numbers so they divide exactly without
remainders.

Tackling the Exercise
This work requires no new skills, just enough persistence to
keep plodding through the method. If your child is worried
that she's working too slowly, reassure her that everyone takes
a long time to answer questions like these.

The only real complication will come if your child is trying
to show the working in the traditional way. For question 2, the
method works like this:

a) How many seventeens in two?
   None, so change the two thousands into twenty hundreds
   to give a total of twenty-four hundreds.

b) How many seventeens in twenty-four?

One and seven left over. Change the seven hundreds into seventy tens to give a total of seventy-three tens.

Write this as:

$$\frac{1}{17)\overline{24^731}} \qquad \begin{array}{r} 24 \\ -17 \\ \hline 7 \end{array}$$

or:

$$17)\overline{\begin{array}{c} 1 \\ 24^731 \\ 17 \\ \hline 7 \end{array}}$$

If your child is using the second method, she may prefer to write a three at the bottom beside the seven instead of putting a small seven beside the three in the original number. This is fine provided she understands what she's doing but don't use the phrase 'bring down the three' because that doesn't explain what's happening.

c) How many seventeens in seventy-three?

Four and five left over.

Write down the four and turn the five tens left over into fifty ones to make a total of fifty-one ones.

Write this as:

$$17)\overline{\begin{array}{c} 1\ 4 \\ 24^73^51 \end{array}} \qquad \begin{array}{r} 24 \\ -17 \\ \hline 7 \end{array} \qquad \begin{array}{r} 17 \\ \times 5 \\ \hline 85 \end{array} \qquad \begin{array}{r} 17 \\ \times 4 \\ \hline 68 \end{array} \qquad \begin{array}{r} 73 \\ -68 \\ \hline 5 \end{array}$$

or:

```
            1 4
    17) 2 4 ⁷3 ⁵1        1 7      1 7
        1 7              x 5      x 4
        ———              ——       ——
          7 3            8 5      6 8
          6 8
          ———
            5
```

d) How many seventeens are there in fifty–one?
   Exactly three so the answer is 143.
   Write this as:

```
         1 4 3        2 4      1 7    1 7    7 3     1 7
    17) 2 4 ⁷3 ⁵1    -1 7     x 5    x 4   -6 8    x 3
                      ——       ——     ——     ——     ——
                        7      8 5    6 8      5    5 1
```

or

```
          1 4 3
    17) 2 4 ⁷3 ⁵1       1 7      1 7      1 7
        1 7             x 5      x 4      x 3
        ———             ——       ——       ——
          7 3           8 5      6 8      5 1
          6 8
          ———
          5 1
```

Moving On

Stay on this level until your child is confident with this type of question and can answer them accurately. Then move on to another topic.

27 / Measurement

Imagine you've got three hamsters, four canaries and an overwhelming desire to do some maths. You can't say you have seven hamsters or seven canaries because it just wouldn't be true. Hamsters and canaries are different. But they're both pets so you can say you have seven pets.

Measurements are like that too. You can only do maths with them if they're all measured in the same units. So one kilogram and one gram added together are neither two kilograms nor two grams. To add them properly, we have to either change the kilogram to grams:

$$1000 \text{ g} + 1 \text{ g} = 1001 \text{ g}$$

or change the grams to kilograms:

$$1 \text{ kg} + 0{\cdot}001 \text{ kg} = 1{\cdot}001 \text{ kg}$$

Provided all the measurements are in the same units, questions involving measurements are no more complicated than equivalent ones using ordinary numbers. Your child doesn't need any extra skills to tackle them, so if he knows that $6 + 4 = 10$, he also knows that 6 cm + 4 cm = 10 cm.

IMPORTANT
The answer to 6 cm + 4 cm is 10 cm, not 10. It's vitally important that your child always writes the correct units after his answer when he's working with measurements. If he doesn't do so in a test, he'll lose marks even if the actual numbers are right.

Metric or Imperial Units

It's essential that your child understands metric units (metres, kilograms, etcetera) as these are the ones he'll use in all his subjects at school. Always let him use them whenever he measures anything with you at home.

However, imperial units haven't completely died out. In Britain distances are still measured in miles, milk still comes in pint containers and apples are still priced at so much per pound. To cope with everyday life your child needs a rough idea of how these units relate to the metric ones he uses most of the time. For instance, one litre is a bit less than two pints while one kilogram is slightly more than two pounds.

Understanding Measurement

Encourage your child to look at the labels on the packets and jars you buy. Talk about whether the contents are being sold by their length, their weight or by the amount of space they take up (in other words, their volume). Help him to notice which units are used for each type of measurement.

Try to involve him in any practical measuring you do during cooking, sewing, gardening or other activities. This will help him develop an idea of how big the units are, especially if you both try to guess the size before you measure it.

CHANGING UNITS

In order to tackle questions where the measurements are not all given in the same units, your child needs to be able to change from one unit to another.

Essential Background Knowledge
Before starting this topic, your child should:

a) know the names of the metric units and how they relate to each other (for example, 100 cm = 1 metre, 1000 g = 1 kg)
b) understand decimals and be able to use them confidently
c) be able to multiply and divide by ten, a hundred and a thousand (see chapter 23).

Before You Start the Session
Write this exercise in your child's book:

1)	1 kg	=	g	11)	100 m	=	km
2)	3 kg	=	g	12)	4000 m	=	km
3)	7·24 km	=	m	13)	500 ml	=	l
4)	5 km	=	m	14)	1340 ml	=	l
5)	4·04 km	=	m	15)	750 g	=	kg
6)	4 l	=	ml	16)	1500 kg	=	kg
7)	6·3 l	=	m	17)	175 cm	=	m
8)	3 m	=	cm	18)	60 cm	=	m
9)	7·1 m	=	cm	19)	8 mm	=	cm
10)	4 cm	=	mm	20)	20 mm	=	cm

To write more exercises, make up similar questions asking your child to change from small units to large ones or from large units to small ones.

Tackling the Exercise
These questions are straightforward provided your child can remember how the units relate to each other and how to multiply by ten, a hundred and a thousand. Be prepared to remind him if he has forgotten and, if necessary, reassure him that everyone forgets sometimes. He may like to have the relationship between the units written down on a sheet of paper which he can look at if he needs to.

Moving On
Stay on this level until your child can change from one size of
unit to another without difficulty. Then move on to a different
topic.

AREA

Area is the space taken up by a flat shape. We measure it by the
number of squares of a set size we could fit inside the shape.
With metric measurements, we usually use squares with each
side 1 cm long (square centimetres or cm^2). For larger shapes
we use squares with sides 1 m long (square metres or m^2).

Finding Areas of Rectangles

Essential Background Knowledge
Before your child starts this topic he should:
a) know that area is measured in squares
b) be able to multiply by numbers no larger than ten.

Equipment
You'll need some squared paper. Don't worry if the squares
aren't square centimetres. For this work, you can just use the
side of one square as your unit for length and the squares
themselves as your unit for area.

Tackling the Topic
Draw five rectangles on your squared paper. Make them all
two units high but make the widths three, four, five, six and
seven units respectively. Ask your child to count the squares
and help him write the answers in a table like this:

Length	Width	Area
2	3	12
2	4	16
2	5	20
2	6	24
2	7	28

When he has finished, ask him to look at his answers and see if he notices anything about them. If necessary, help him to see that, for each rectangle, he could find the area by multiplying the length by the width. Then encourage him to use that fact to work out the area of a rectangle two units high and ten units wide and to draw a picture to see if he's right. He can also draw some other pictures to check if the same method works for rectangles of different heights. Make sure he realizes that the method only works for rectangles.

You can then give him the length and width of other rectangles and ask him to work out the areas. Give him the lengths in centimetres or metres and make sure he uses the correct units for his answers. He can use a calculator if the numbers are too awkward for him to multiply easily.

Moving On
Stay on this topic until your child can work out the area of a rectangle confidently with only occasional mistakes. Then move on to another topic.

VOLUME

The volume of an object is the amount of space it takes up. Just as we measure area in squares, we measure volume in cubes: usually cubic centimetres (cc or cm³) or cubic metres (m³). We can also measure the volume of liquids in litres and millilitres: 1 ml and 1 cc are almost exactly the same size so, for all practical purposes, 1000 cc are the same as 1 litre.

Calculating Volumes

The simplest shape for which you can work out the volume is
a cuboid (a rectangular box shape). Your child will understand
and remember the method better if he discovers it for himself
from practical experience using identical cube-shaped bricks. If
you can't get hold of any, he can draw pictures instead.

Essential Background Knowledge
Before tackling this topic your child should:
a) know that volume is measured in cubes
b) be able to work out the area of a rectangle
c) be able to multiply any number by a number no larger than
   ten.

Tackling the Topic
Ask your child to build or draw a single layer of bricks two
wide and three long. This shape is called a cuboid and is one
brick high. Talk about the area of the table which it covers
(six) and how many bricks you have used (six).

Now ask him to add another layer of bricks so the cuboid is
now two bricks high but still covers the same area. How many
bricks has he used?

Ask him the same questions again as he adds a third layer and
a fourth and then help him write his answers in a table like this:

Length	Width	Area of Base	Height	Volume
2	3	6	1	6
2	3	6	2	12
2	3	6	3	18
2	3	6	4	24

Help your child to see from the table that he could work out
the volume by multiplying the area of the base by the height.

Let him repeat the same process using different numbers of

bricks for the bottom layer to see if this relationship is always true. If he wishes, he can try arranging the bottom layer of bricks in a shape which isn't a rectangle (a cross perhaps or an L-shape). He'll find he can still work out the volume by multiplying the area by the height.

Once he understands this method, help him to practise it by giving him the sizes of some cuboids and asking him to work out their volumes. Let him use a calculator if the numbers are too awkward to multiply easily.

But I was taught that the volume of a cuboid was length × width × height.

Although these two methods may look different, they're not. Because the area of a rectangle is the length times the width, working out length × width × height is exactly the same as working out base area × height. The advantage with the method I suggest is that it works for some other shapes too (like cylinders), so it gives your child a better foundation for the work he'll meet later on.

Moving On

Stay on this level until your child can confidently work out the volume of a cuboid without help. Then move on to another topic.

If I want to know if I can afford three T-shirts for £8·99 each, I can save myself some hard work by thinking of the price as if it were £9 instead. The answer won't be quite accurate but it'll be near enough to tell me what I need to know.

Rough answers like this are very useful in real life. They depend on changing a number to one which is nearly the same size but easier to work with. This process is called 'rounding' (or sometimes 'correcting'). In the previous example we rounded £8·99 to the nearest whole number.

ROUNDING NUMBERS

Essential Background Knowledge
Your child must be able to count forwards and backwards confidently before she starts this topic.

Step 1

Aim
To introduce rounding numbers to the nearest ten.

Before You Start the Session
Write this exercise in your child's book:

1)	73	5)	34
2)	29	6)	75
3)	65	7)	81
4)	86	8)	25

9)	39	14)	455
10)	141	15)	115
11)	289	19)	99
12)	135	17)	154
13)	439	18)	41

To write more exercises, write down whole numbers which don't have a zero in the ones position and ask your child to round them to the nearest ten.

Tackling the Exercise

When you've finished the oral work, tell your child the real life example of rounding from the beginning of the chapter or make up another of your own. Explain that we sometimes need to change a number to one that is easier to use. If we change to a number which is a little bigger, we say we have rounded it up. If we choose one which is a bit smaller, we say we have rounded it down.

Then show her the exercise and explain that you want her to round the numbers up or down to the nearest ten. Look at the first question together and ask her whether seventy-three is nearer to seventy or eighty. When she chooses seventy, explain that seventy-three rounded to the nearest ten is seventy. Let her write the answer next to the seventy-three (without an equals sign as they're not equal: she can put a space or an arrow instead). Continue to help her in this way for as long as necessary.

Question 3 brings an added complication: sixty-five is exactly halfway between sixty and seventy. Explain that mathematicians have agreed that, when this happens, we always round the number up. So sixty-five rounded to the nearest ten is seventy.

Moving On

Keep practising this process until your child can confidently round any whole number to the nearest ten. Then move on to step 2.

Step 2

Aim
To introduce rounding to the nearest hundred.

Before You Start the Session
Write this exercise in your child's book:

1)	190	9)	4762
2)	210	10)	3521
3)	563	11)	5631
4)	750	12)	3567
5)	325	13)	7450
6)	450	14)	9876
7)	762	15)	1350
8)	112	16)	490

To write more exercises, write down numbers greater than a hundred for your child to round to the nearest hundred.

Tackling the Exercise
Work with your child until she understands what to do. Help her to see that rounding to the nearest hundred is a very similar process to rounding to the nearest ten, only this time she has to decide which hundred the number is nearest to.

So in the first two questions 190 rounds up to 200 and 210 rounds down to 200. As before, she should round the number up if it lies exactly halfway between the two choices so, in question 4, 750 rounds up to 800.

Moving On
Stay on this level until your child can easily round any number to the nearest hundred. Then move on to a new topic or tackle the suggested further work.

Further Work
Once your child has finished steps 1 and 2, try rounding larger numbers to the nearest thousand, ten thousand or even to the nearest million.

If she's confident with decimals, you can also ask her to practise rounding (or correcting) decimal numbers to the nearest whole number (5·64 becomes 6, 7·39 becomes 7, 2·5 becomes 3 and so on).

RESTRICTING THE NUMBER OF DECIMAL PLACES

Essential Background Knowledge
Before tackling this topic, your child should:
a) be able to use decimals confidently
a) be able to round numbers up or down.

Tackling the Topic
Suppose you want to divide a piece of string 58 cm long into seven equal pieces. Your calculator will tell you that each piece should be 8·2857142 cm long but there's no way you can measure string as accurately as that. You need an answer with only one number after the decimal point. The way to get that is to round the answer to the nearest tenth so 8·2857142 becomes 8·3. This process is called correcting the number to one decimal place.

If you wanted the answer to have two numbers after the decimal point, you would have to round it to the nearest hundredth. Then 8·2857142 would become 8·29. This is called correcting the number to two decimal places.

To help your child practise this process, write down numbers which have several figures after the decimal point and ask her to correct them to one or two decimal places. If you prefer, you can show her the numbers one at a time on a calculator display. This will add variety to your work and fit the task into the situation where she's most likely to use it.

REMEMBER
- **To correct a number to one decimal place, round it to the nearest tenth**
- **To correct a number to two decimal places, round it to the nearest hundredth**

ESTIMATING ANSWERS

Rough answers or educated guesses are useful in maths because they can help us spot mistakes but mathematicians prefer to call them estimates or approximations. (Although they are lazy, they love long words.)

Estimating the answer to a question is especially valuable when you're using a calculator. Although this miracle of modern technology can work out arithmetic with ease, its ability to tell you the right answer is dependent on your ability to ask it the right question. (This fact is known to computer programmers as garbage in = garbage out.)

It's very easy to press the wrong button without realizing it, so the calculator is working with the wrong numbers or adding when it should be dividing. This often produces an answer which is wildly wrong so, if you've a rough idea of the answer you're expecting, you'll usually spot your mistake.

Practising Estimation

Essential Background Skills
Before your child starts this topic she should:
a) be able to round numbers up and down
b) be able to work out simple calculations, for example:

$$500 - 300, 100 \div 2, 200 \times 3, \quad 400 + 500.$$

Before You Start the Session

Write this exercise in your child's book:

1)	376 + 492 = 1318	6)	59 × 5 = 295
	376 + 492 = 868		59 × 5 = 472
2)	203 − 94 = 297	7)	192 − 67 = 125
	203 − 94 = 109		192 − 67 = 259
3)	912 − 364 = 548	8)	1224 ÷ 18 = 153
	912 − 364 = 1276		1224 ÷ 18 = 68
4)	318 × 2 = 159	9)	76 × 9 = 684
	318 × 2 = 636		76 × 9 = 85
5)	465 × 3 = 155	10)	51 × 99 = 459
	465 × 3 = 1395		51 × 99 = 5049

To write more exercises, make up similar questions which are too difficult to work out easily without a calculator. Write each question twice: once with the right answer and once with a wrong answer obtained by making a deliberate mistake with the calculator. Make sure the wrong answer is substantially different from the right one and vary putting the right answer first or second.

Tackling the Topic

When you show your child the exercise, explain that each question is written once with the right answer and once with the wrong one. Her task is to decide which answer is correct without working out the question herself. She just needs to work out the answer roughly (in mathematical terms make an estimate) and she'll be able to spot which one is wrong.

Be prepared to work with her until she understands what to do. For the first question, encourage her to round 376 to 400 and 492 to 500. If she then adds 400 to 500 to get an estimate of 376 + 492, she'll easily spot the wrong answer.

Continue to work with her until she has the confidence to work alone. Be ready to step in quickly if she rounds a number incorrectly but remember that there may be more than one way of tackling some of the questions. For instance, you could simplify question 7 to 200 − 100 or 190 − 70. Both methods are equally correct.

Moving On

Keep practising this type of exercise until your child can easily estimate answers. Then move on to another topic but, whenever she uses a calculator, encourage her to use estimation to check if her answer is sensible.

29 / Tackling Written Questions

Throughout this book we've avoided using words in the written work. This has allowed your child to gain confidence and skill with numbers without having to worry about reading. His only contact with maths described in words has been through your oral work together, especially the number stories.

However teachers and textbooks delight in asking questions about supposedly genuine situations instead of just giving children numbers to add, subtract, multiply and divide. This is supposed to make maths realistic but unfortunately these written questions don't just add realism. They add complications especially if your child's reading skills are still not well developed. Long words and unusual sentence construction may prove so difficult to understand that he can't find his way through them to the maths.

HELPING WITH WRITTEN QUESTIONS

When you're helping your child with a question written in words, try working through the following stages together.

1) Make sure he can read and understand all the words in the question. If there are words neither of you understand, help your child look them up in a dictionary or in the glossary of this book.
2) Encourage him to read through the question carefully to decide what he's being asked to find.
3) Help him to find all the information which is given in the

question. Writing this information down will sometimes help him sort out the maths from the words. If the question involves a shape, encourage him to draw a rough sketch of it and mark on the lengths he knows.

4) Encourage him to look at the information and try to decide how to use it to find the answer. Remember that maths questions hardly ever contain numbers you don't need. If he's been told a number, he probably needs to use it to find the answer.

5) If your child can't see what to do but you can, try rephrasing the question into an 'I think of a number' puzzle. For instance, suppose the question is about a garden with four sides. The distance round the outside of the garden is 36 m. The lengths of three of the sides are 10m, 8m, and 6m. How long is the fourth side? Your conversation might sound like this:

YOU: Suppose you knew how long the fourth side was. How could you find the distance round the outside of the garden?

CHILD: I already know it.

YOU: But suppose you didn't. Suppose it was that distance you had to find? How could you do it?

CHILD: I could add all the four sides together.

YOU: So the side we don't know added to all the others tells us the distance round the outside.

CHILD: Yes.

YOU: And that distance round the outside is . . .?

CHILD: Thirty-six metres.

YOU: Good. So we know that if we add the fourth side to the three we already know, the answer's thirty-six metres.

CHILD: Does that help?

YOU: It will eventually. Now what's the answer if we just add the three sides we know together?

CHILD: Twenty-four.

YOU: Twenty-four what?

CHILD: Twenty-four metres.

YOU: That's right. So if we add the fourth side to twenty-four metres, the answer is thirty-six metres, isn't it?

CHILD: Yes.

YOU: Suppose I think of a number. I add twenty-four and the answer's thirty-six. What's the number?

CHILD: Twelve.

YOU: So, how long is that fourth side if when I add twenty-four metres to it, the answer's thirty-six metres?

CHILD: Twelve metres.

YOU: Well done.

6) If neither of you can see how to tackle the question, encourage your child to ask his teacher for help. Remember there's no shame in getting stuck sometimes. Even teachers occasionally meet questions they can't answer and it's not unknown for a mistake in a question to make it impossible.

Proportion Questions

Maths teachers are very fond of situations where one amount is dependent on (or in proportion to) another. Questions like 'If one pencil costs 5p, how much do three pencils cost?' involve what is called direct proportion because the cost gets bigger when more items are bought and smaller when fewer items are bought. Direct proportion is important in maths and in real life. For instance, the amount of food you need is directly proportional to the number of people you're feeding and the distance travelled by a car is directly proportional to its speed.

Maths questions also sometimes involve inverse proportion where one amount becomes smaller as another becomes larger. Inverse proportion is popular with maths teachers, much less popular with their pupils and not all that common in real life.

One example of it is the way the time taken to do a job goes down when the number of people working on it goes up. That's why your memories of school maths probably include a surprisingly large amount of time thinking about men digging holes.

Your child doesn't need to memorize a set technique for solving proportion questions. It's far less confusing for him to work out the answer to each one using common sense and his basic knowledge of maths. To show you what I mean, I'll work through two questions with you.

Question 1 Direct Proportion
    Seven pencils cost 35p. How much do nine cost?

Cost of 7 pencils = 35p
Cost of 1 pencil = 35 ÷ 7 = 5p

(You know you need to divide because one pencil will cost less than seven.)

Cost of 9 pencils = 9 × 5 = 45p

(You know you need to multiply because nine pencils will cost more than one.)

Question 2 Inverse Proportion
    Three people paint a wall in ninety minutes. How long would five people working at the same speed have taken to paint the wall.

3 people take 90 minutes
1 person takes 90 × 3 = 270 minutes

(You multiply this time because one person will take longer.)

5 people take 270 ÷ 5 = 54 minutes

(You divide this time because five people will take less time.)

Glossary

ARITHMETIC: the traditional name for number work. Addition, subtraction, multiplication and division are sometimes called the four rules of arithmetic.

AVERAGE: one number chosen to represent a group of several numbers. The most commonly used average is the MEAN but your child may also learn about the MEDIAN and the MODE.

CALCULATE: work out.

CUBE: a) a solid shape with six sides, all of which are squares. It is a special type of cuboid.
b) a number multiplied by itself three times, so the cube of 5 is $5 \times 5 \times 5$ which is often written as 5^3.

CUBOID: a solid shape like a cereal packet or matchbox. Each side is a rectangle and the opposite pairs of sides are the same size.

DATA: information, particularly the type of information gathered from surveys and investigations.

DATA HANDLING: sorting information into a useful form and displaying it in tables, graphs and charts.

DENOMINATOR: the bottom number of a fraction.

DIGIT: an individual numeral which makes up a larger number. So 2, 5 and 8 are the digits in the number 258.

EQUILATERAL TRIANGLE: A triangle which has all its sides the same length and all its angles equal to each other.

EVEN NUMBER: a number which can be divided exactly by two. 4, 12, and 122 are all even numbers.

FACTOR: a number which will divide exactly into another number. 3 is a factor of 12 and 7 is a factor of 28.

FIGURE: a) another word for a digit. In the number 3576, the figures are 3, 5, 7 and 6.
b) another word for a diagram.

HEXAGON: any shape with six straight sides.

ISOSCELES TRIANGLE: a triangle with two of its sides the same length. The angles between these sides and the third side are both the same size.

MEAN: the average of a group of numbers worked out by adding all the numbers together and dividing the total by the number in the group. For the group 4, 6, 5, 7, 3 and 5, the total is 30 so the mean is $30 \div 6$ which is 5.

MEDIAN:
the average of a group of numbers found by arranging them in numerical order. The number in the middle is the median. So for the group 3, 4, 5, 8, 10, 12 and 16, the median is 8.

MODE:
the average of a group of numbers found by deciding which number occurs most frequently. So for the group 3, 3, 6, 6, 6, 7 and 9, the mode is 6.

MULTIPLE:
a number made by multiplying another number. So 6 is a multiple of 2 and 20 is a multiple of 10.

NEGATIVE NUMBERS:
all the numbers which are smaller than zero. They occur in real life when we measure temperatures below freezing and the best way to introduce them to your child is by looking at a thermometer.

NUMBER BOND:
a fact which connects numbers together. The facts $3 + 4 = 7$ and $6 - 2 = 4$ are both number bonds.

NUMERATOR:
the top number of a fraction.

OBLONG:
the common name for a rectangle. It is not usually used in maths.

OCTAGON:
any shape with eight straight sides.

ODD NUMBER:
a number which cannot be divided exactly by two. 3, 7 and 93 are all odd numbers.

PENTAGON:
any shape with five straight sides.

PERIMETER:
the distance round the outside of a flat shape.

PRIME NUMBER: a number which cannot be divided exactly by any number except itself and one. 2, 3, 7 and 11 are all prime numbers.

QUADRILATERAL: any shape with four straight sides.

RECTANGLE: a special type of quadrilateral where all the angles are right angles and the opposite pairs of sides are equal in length.

REGULAR: a regular shape is one which has all its sides the same length.

SQUARE: a) a special type of rectangle where all the sides are the same length.
b) a number multiplied by itself. The square of 5 is 5×5 which is often written as 5^2.

SUM: a) the result of adding numbers together. So the sum of 2 and 3 is 5.
b) another name for an arithmetic question.

TRIANGLE: any shape with three straight sides.

UNIT: a quantity chosen as a standard measurement which we can use to describe other measurements. An hour is a unit of time and a metre is a unit of length.

Index

Discover more about our forthcoming books through Penguin's FREE newspaper...

It's packed with:

- exciting features
- author interviews
- previews & reviews
- books from your favourite films & TV series
- exclusive competitions & much, much more...

Write off for your free copy today to:
Dept JC
Penguin Books Ltd
FREEPOST
West Drayton
Middlesex
UB7 0BR
NO STAMP REQUIRED

READ MORE IN PENGUIN

In every corner of the world, on every subject under the sun, Penguin represents quality and variety – the very best in publishing today.

For complete information about books available from Penguin – including Puffins, Penguin Classics and Arkana – and how to order them, write to us at the appropriate address below. Please note that for copyright reasons the selection of books varies from country to country.

In the United Kingdom: Please write to *Dept. JC, Penguin Books Ltd, FREEPOST, West Drayton, Middlesex UB7 OBR.*

If you have any difficulty in obtaining a title, please send your order with the correct money, plus ten per cent for postage and packaging, to *PO Box No. 11, West Drayton, Middlesex UB7 OBR*

In the United States: Please write to *Consumer Sales, Penguin USA, P.O. Box 999, Dept. 17109, Bergenfield, New Jersey 07621-0120.* VISA and MasterCard holders call 1-800-253-6476 to order all Penguin titles

In Canada: Please write to *Penguin Books Canada Ltd, 10 Alcorn Avenue, Suite 300, Toronto, Ontario M4V 3B2*

In Australia: Please write to *Penguin Books Australia Ltd, P.O. Box 257, Ringwood, Victoria 3134*

In New Zealand: Please write to *Penguin Books (NZ) Ltd, Private Bag 102902, North Shore Mail Centre, Auckland 10*

In India: Please write to *Penguin Books India Pvt Ltd, 706 Eros Apartments, 56 Nehru Place, New Delhi 110 019*

In the Netherlands: Please write to *Penguin Books Netherlands bv, Postbus 3507, NL-1001 AH Amsterdam*

In Germany: Please write to *Penguin Books Deutschland GmbH, Metzlerstrasse 26, 60594 Frankfurt am Main*

In Spain: Please write to *Penguin Books S. A., Bravo Murillo 19, 1° B, 28015 Madrid*

In Italy: Please write to *Penguin Italia s.r.l., Via Felice Casati 20, I–20124 Milano*

In France: Please write to *Penguin France S. A., 17 rue Lejeune, F–31000 Toulouse*

In Japan: Please write to *Penguin Books Japan, Ishikiribashi Building, 2–5–4, Suido, Bunkyo-ku, Tokyo 112*

In Greece: Please write to *Penguin Hellas Ltd, Dimocritou 3, GR–106 71 Athens*

In South Africa: Please write to *Longman Penguin Southern Africa (Pty) Ltd, Private Bag X08, Bertsham 2013*

READ MORE IN PENGUIN

SCIENCE AND MATHEMATICS

The Character of Physical Law   Richard P. Feynman

'Richard Feynman had both genius and highly unconventional style . . .
His contributions touched almost every corner of the subject, and have had
a deep and abiding influence over the way that physicists think' – Paul
Davies

Fearful Symmetry   Ian Stewart and Martin Golubitsky

'Symmetry-breaking is an important unifying idea in modern abstract
mathematics, so it's a tribute to the authors' expository gifts that much of
the book reads like a captivating travelogue' – *The New York Times Book
Review*

Bully for Brontosaurus   Stephen Jay Gould

'He fossicks through history, here and there picking up a bone, an imprint,
a fossil dropping, and, from these, tries to reconstruct the past afresh in all
its messy ambiguity. It's the droppings that provide the freshness: he's as
likely to quote from Mark Twain or Joe DiMaggio as from Lamarck or
Lavoisier' – *Guardian*

Are We Alone?   Paul Davies

Since ancient times people have been fascinated by the idea of
extraterrestrial life; today we are searching systematically for it. Paul
Davies's striking new book examines the assumptions that go into this
search and draws out the startling implications for science, religion and our
world view, should we discover that we are not alone.

The Making of the Atomic Bomb   Richard Rhodes

'Rhodes handles his rich trove of material with the skill of a master
novelist . . . his portraits of the leading figures are three-dimensional and
penetrating . . . the sheer momentum of the narrative is breathtaking . . . a
book to read and to read again' – *Guardian*

READ MORE IN PENGUIN

SCIENCE AND MATHEMATICS

Bright Air, Brilliant Fire   Gerald Edelman

'A brilliant and captivating new vision of the mind' – Oliver Sacks. 'Every page of Edelman's huge wok of a book crackles with delicious ideas, mostly from the *nouvelle cuisine* of neuroscience, but spiced with a good deal of intellectual history, with side dishes on everything from schizophrenia to embryology' – *The Times*

Games of Life   Karl Sigmund
Explorations in Ecology, Evolution and Behaviour

'A beautifully written and, considering its relative brevity, amazingly comprehensive survey of past and current thinking in "mathematical" evolution . . . Just as games are supposed to be fun, so too is *Games of Life*' – *The Times Higher Education Supplement*

Gödel, Escher, Bach: An Eternal Golden Braid
Douglas F. Hofstadter

'Every few decades an unknown author brings out a book of such depth, clarity, range, wit, beauty and originality that it is recognized at once as a major literary event' – Martin Gardner. 'Leaves you feeling you have had a first-class workout in the best mental gymnasium in town' – *New Statesman*

The Doctrine of DNA   R. C. Lewontin

'He is the most brilliant scientist I know and his work embodies, as this book displays so well, the very best in genetics, combined with a powerful political and moral vision of how science, properly interpreted and used to empower all the people, might truly help us to be free' – Stephen Jay Gould

Artificial Life   Steven Levy

'Can an engineered creation be alive? This centuries-old question is the starting point for Steven Levy's lucid book . . . *Artificial Life* is not only exhilarating reading but an all-too-rare case of a scientific popularization that breaks important new ground' – *The New York Times Book Review*

READ MORE IN PENGUIN

SCIENCE AND MATHEMATICS

The Edge of Infinity   Paul Davies

Over the past decade, the evidence for black holes has greatly increased. In this updated edition, Paul Davies considers the latest research in this exciting and rapidly-developing field. At issue is the existence of boundaries not only to the physical universe, but maybe also to the very idea of what can be known and understood.

The Newtonian Casino   Thomas A. Bass

'The story's appeal lies in its romantic obsessions ... Post-hippie computer freaks develop a system to beat the System, and take on Las Vegas to heroic and thrilling effect' – *The Times*

Wonderful Life   Stephen Jay Gould

'He weaves together three extraordinary themes – one palaeontological, one human, one theoretical and historical – as he discusses the discovery of the Burgess Shale, with its amazing, wonderfully preserved fossils – a time-capsule of the early Cambrian seas' – *Mail on Sunday*

The *New Scientist* Guide to Chaos   Edited by Nina Hall

In this collection of incisive reports, acknowledged experts such as Ian Stewart, Robert May and Benoit Mandelbrot draw on the latest research to explain the roots of chaos in modern mathematics and physics.

Innumeracy   John Allen Paulos

'An engaging compilation of anecdotes and observations about those circumstances in which a very simple piece of mathematical insight can save an awful lot of futility' – *The Times Educational Supplement*

Fractals   Hans Lauwerier

The extraordinary visual beauty of fractal images and their applications in chaos theory have made these endlessly repeating geometric figures widely familiar. This invaluable new book makes clear the basic mathematics of fractals; it will also teach people with computers how to make fractals themselves.